Rebecca Weaver Hunt

Casper Mountain Ski History

A COMMUNITY OF SKIERS

THE
DONNING COMPANY
PUBLISHERS

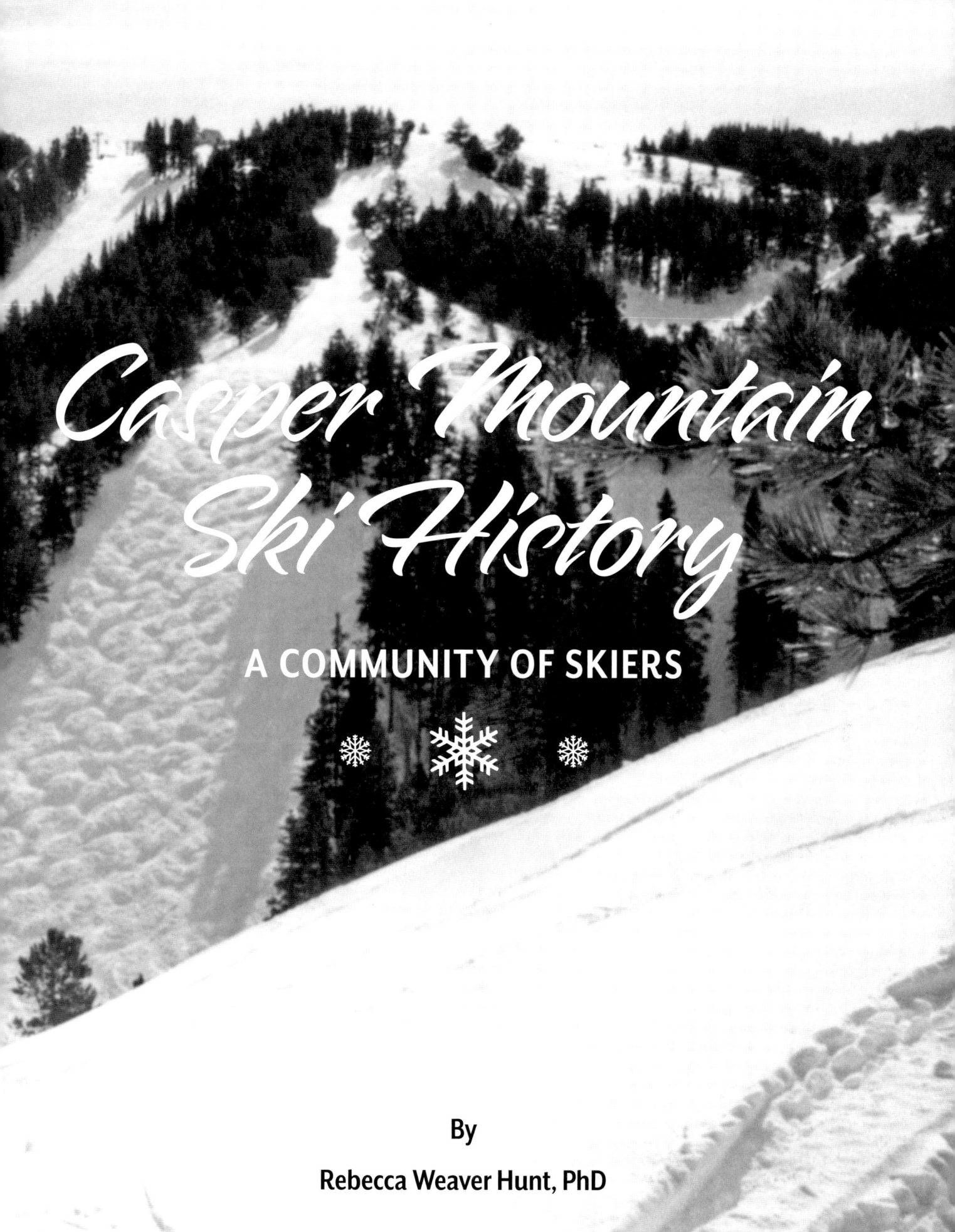

Casper Mountain Ski History

A COMMUNITY OF SKIERS

❄ ❄ ❄

By

Rebecca Weaver Hunt, PhD

Front cover: **Spectators and competitors on Casper ski run, 1930s**

Back cover, clockwise from the top left:

Hardesty on the Miner/Spillway tow

The Casper Race

Cross-country skis on a groomed trail

Bochmann art – New lodge and skiers

(Photographs courtesy of Glenn Bochmann)

The Donning Company Publishers
731 South Brunswick Street
Brookfield, MO 64628

Lex Cavanah, *General Manager*
Nathan Stufflebean, *Production Supervisor*
Philip Briscoe, *Editor*
Stephanie L. Danko, *Graphic Designer*
Katie Gardner, *Marketing and Project Coordinator*
Brooke Lauhoff, *Project Research Coordinator*

Cathleen Norman, *Project Director*

Library of Congress Cataloging-in-Publication Data
Names: Hunt, Rebecca A., 1952- author.
Title: Casper Mountain ski history : a community of skiers / By Rebecca Weaver Hunt, PhD.
Description: Brookfield : The Donning Company Publishers, [2021] | Includes
   bibliographical references and index. | Summary: "A pictorial history of the skiing
   community of Casper Mountain, located in Natrona County, Wyoming"– Provided by publisher.
Identifiers: LCCN 2021046857 | ISBN 9781681843179 (paperback)
Subjects: LCSH: Skis and skiing—Wyoming—Pictorial works. | Casper Mountain
   (Wyo. : Mountain)—Pictorial works.
Classification: LCC GV854.5.W82 H86 2021 | DDC 796.9309787—dc23
LC record available at https://lccn.loc.gov/2021046857

Printed in the United States of America at Walsworth

Table of Contents

Dedication

THIS PROJECT BEGAN AS THE DREAM OF A BUNCH of Casper ski enthusiasts who wanted to document the history of skiing on Casper Mountain in Wyoming. As the idea of the project evolved, they realized that they had to do something to gather the stories of those who were there in the beginning and who were in danger of dying before we could save their stories.

This led to an oral history project, begun in 2008. The members were Pinky and Jackie Ellis, Sean Ellis, MaryAnn Hoff, Rebecca Hunt, Bob Kidd, Sandy Leotta, and Sam Weaver, all founders of the Casper Mountain Ski History Group. They trained to become oral historians, wrote grants, acquired equipment, and began to interview people—first, those who were the eldest of the original ski bunch, and later, others who were part of younger generations. In all, they interviewed over forty people, using both audio and video devices

Sam Weaver, 2018 *(Laurie Weaver collection)*

to record each interview. The next step was the painstaking transcription of the interviews. A number of the interviewees have since died, but their stories live on.

We dedicate this book to all of those who imagined and lived the dream of skiing on Casper Mountain, and to those who did the hard work to make the dream a reality. Finally, we dedicate it to the memory of Sam Weaver, who did so much to bring the project into being but who left us too early, in March of 2018. We carry on in his name.

—The Casper Mountain Ski History Team

The team at work, 2010 *(Laurie Weaver collection)*

Foreword

*M*OST SKI HISTORIES DOCUMENT THE EFFORTS and successes of a single individual to create a mountain ski empire. This is true of Vail, Steamboat, and Loveland, all in Colorado. Our story on Casper Mountain skiing is a very different kind of tale.

Wyoming is sparsely populated, and most of the big endeavors have been the product of community effort. This was true in the early territorial and state days of Wyoming, and it was also true as people moved to—and created—Natrona County and its institutions.

One of our great treasures is our mountain. It has offered recreation from the beginning. Skiing came early and grew, slowly at first, but then exponentially faster as Casper boomed after World War II. Seasoned mountaineers and new arrivals teamed up to take a fledgling collection of ski hills and, with the addition of Hogadon Ski Area, turn the mountain into a destination for generations of ski aficionados. So, this is a story not of individual enterprise, but of group dreams made real through group enterprise. Our Casper Mountain ski story is a community story that resonates to this day.

Acknowledgements

*J*UST LIKE THE STORY OF SKIING ON CASPER Mountain, this book is the product of a community effort. We have been unusually blessed with sources. The committee undertook the daunting task of gathering over forty oral histories. They used audio and video devices to document the process. Our team has been Sam Weaver, Sandy Leotta, MaryAnn Hoff, Bob Kidd, Sean Ellis, Pinky Ellis, Jackie Ellis, and Ryan Butler. In the past three years, Sean Ellis has been our fearless leader as committee chair. Rebecca Hunt is the author. Barbara Bogart, a Wyoming oral historian, transcribed the interviews. Jacek Bugocki is our amazing documentarian. We would also like to thank two academic peer reviewers, James Whiteside, PhD, and Geoffrey Hunt, PhD, who each read countless drafts of the manuscript and gave tough—but needed—advice.

The community shared numerous photos and other research materials. Fred Walters of Longmont, Colorado, donated newspaper clippings related to early ski races. Julie York gave us stories, clippings, and photos of her family's roles in ski development. The Weaver family saved thirty years of the diaries of Ole Fougstedt, who nurtured young skiers and tended ski tows from the 1930s into the 1950s. The Weavers also saved minutes of meetings, documents from races, and much of the minutia of the Casper Mountain Ski Patrol. Glenn Bochmann shot and labeled many excellent photographs.

Bob Kidd graciously allowed us to use his father's (David Kidd's) home movies. They cover a broad time span that begins in the 1930s. These movies were vital in the creation of our documentary that accompanies the book. Marla Wold and Dick and Dode Perkins also had movies to share.

Chuck Morrison was an early skier and photographer for the *Casper Star-Tribune* for many decades. His photo collections are saved in the Western History Center at Casper College. The History Center staff provided us with clippings, photos, and other sources. They also agreed to be the final repository of our research materials. Thank you to Vince Crolla, Johanna Wickman, and their staff. Below are other community members who helped make this project possible.

Kevin Anderson
Cathy Becker
Susan Bishop
Glenn Bochmann
Barbara Bogart
Rene Bovee
Marty Brammer
Dorothy and Mike Bullard
Arik Christensen
Vince Crolla
Lou and Jan Demorest
Doug French
Greg Irwin

Steve Johnson
Bob and Nancy Kidd
Fred Klein
Donna Loghry
Lance Madzey
Mountain States Publishing Co.
Gay and Sandy Nations
Carrie Pardee
Dick and Dode Perkins
Tori Radosevich
Bart Rea
Shawn Rivett
Sally Ann Shumer

Craig Smith
Karen Snyder
Marge Speas/Stuckenhoff family
(Pete and Marla Wold and J. D. Speas)
Nathan Vondra
Johanna Wickman
Della Works
Julie York
Rick Zimmer

Our incredible team sent out many grant requests to foundations and approached individuals who provided the money we needed to pay a publisher, a transcriptionist, an author, and a documentarian. This funding will allow us to not only produce the book but also a documentary, using ski movies, still photographs, and materials that could not be included in the book. The donors are listed below.

Ralph and Lucille Barton
Bill Bays
Glenn and Pat Bochmann
Barbara Bogart
City of Casper
Casper Mountain Ski Patrol
Bill and Jan Chambers
Colby Drechsler
Jackie and Pinky Ellis
Friends of Hogadon
Keith and Suzanne Garlick
Nancy Gerlock
Goodstein Foundation
Mary Hales

Hardesty Family
Mike Huber
Kemmi Creek Donor Advised
    Endowment Fund
Bob and Nancy Kidd
Bruce and Anne Ladd
Sandy and Miguel Leotta
Sandy Nations
Natrona County Recreation Joint
    Powers Board
Diane and Eric Neste
Rocky Mountain Power Foundation
Arlene Rosen (deceased)
Barbara Scifers (deceased)

Larry and Becky Steensland
Stroock Foundation
Alan Vandeventer
Lesley Waggoner/UW American
    Heritage Center
Warren Memorial Fund
Warren Weaver
Gregg Welton and Christine Haley
Peter and Marla Wold
Wold Foundation
Wyoming Community Foundation -
    donor advised grant
Rick Young/Fort Caspar Museum
Zimmerman Family Trust

Finally, we acknowledge the help of the ski community, especially the Casper Mountain Ski Patrol. Without the patrol's support, we would not be doing this book and documentary. Thank you for caring about our Casper Mountain ski history.

Introduction

THIS IS A HISTORY OF SKIING IN CENTRAL Wyoming from the 1920s to the present. Told through the accounts of ski pioneers and their successors, it is a story of people who dedicated decades of their lives to bringing skiing to Casper Mountain. It chronicles those people, places, and events of skiing on the mountain including now vanished ski runs, the present Hogadon Ski Area, and the extensive cross-country trails. To tell this story, it is important to first look at the origins of skiing in Europe and in the United States.

The Origins of Skiing

Stone Age hunters brought early skis into Northern Europe from the Altai region of central Asia. Craftsmen carved them out of wood and covered the tops with fur. The earliest record of skiing comes from a Swedish petroglyph, dated to B.C.E. 5000 (about 7,000 years ago).[1]

The section below, written by Miles Clark, comes from an article, "The Origins of Skiing," on the website SnowBrains.

> **6300 BC:** The world's oldest skis were discovered in Russia, near Lake Sindor.
>
> **4000 BC:** Rock carvings of a skier from this period were discovered in Norway.
>
> **3300 BC:** Skis from this time period were discovered in Finland. They were 180 centimeters long and 15 centimeters wide. These skis had five grooves.

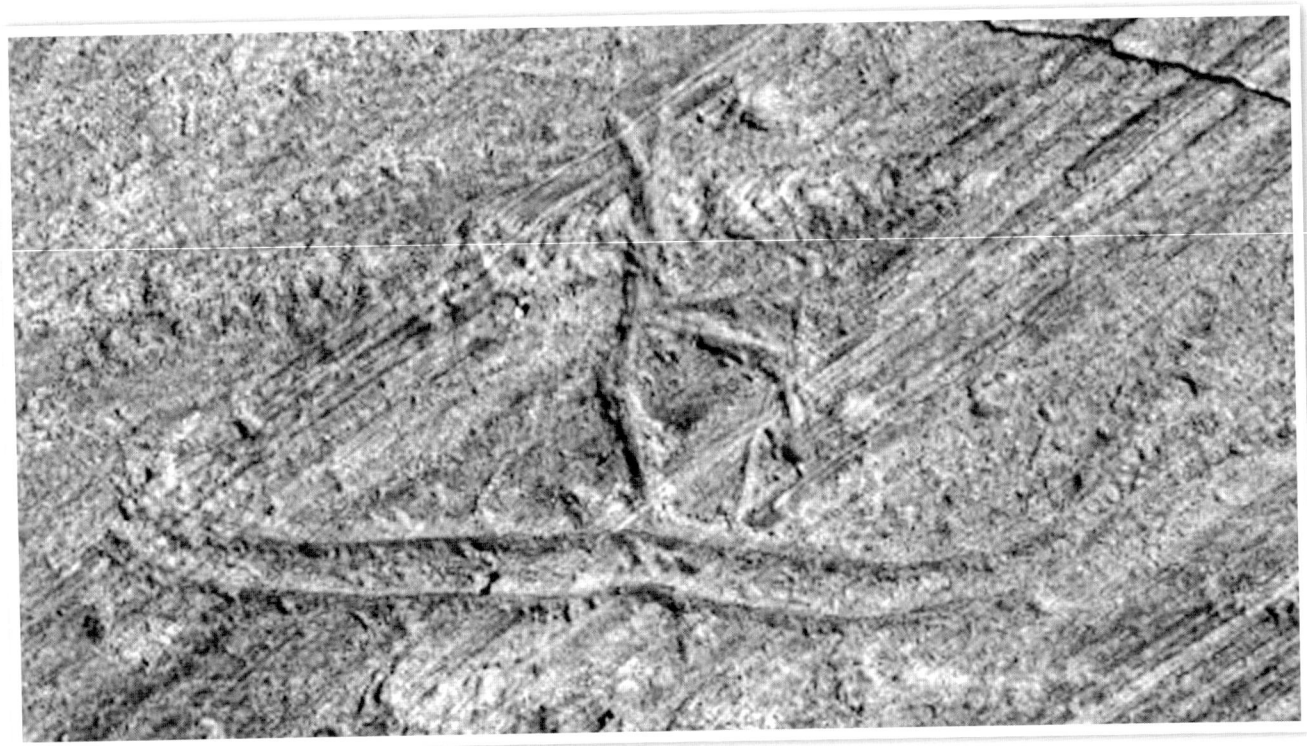

This 5,000-year-old rock carving is the first known image of a human on skis.[2]

2700 BC: Two skis and a pole were dug out of a bog in Sweden.

2500 BC: Archaeologists discovered rock drawings that depict a man on skis holding a stick. The drawings were discovered on a Norwegian island.

200 BC to 200 AD: First documented reference to skiing in China.

The word "ski" comes from the Old Norse word "skíð", which means split piece of firewood.[3] From the invention of skiing in ancient times to modern skiing, there is a myriad of interactions that take place. Skis go from the Sami to the Scandinavians, to the Alps, to the British, to ski racing being started in California and Norway. The amount of information is daunting. For now, we should feel satisfied that we know where skiing first took sprout and grew. In our next installment, we'll explore how skiing morphed from being utilitarian to becoming purely recreational.[4]

In addition to their use by hunters, herders, and travelers, people began to use skis for military transportation. The first documented ski troops were Swedish soldiers from the eighteenth century.[6] A story from Norway told of the secret transport of two-year-old Hååkon Hååkonsson from his home in Lillehammer to Trondheim in 1206. The child was the son of the king of Norway and was in danger of death at the hands of the king's enemies. The king arranged for two of his warriors to hide the child in their backpacks and literally ski for their lives. Prince Haakon's rescuers had skis with the tips curved up, not unlike the prows of Viking longships.

By the 1840s, carvers began to shape skis to resemble a bow with the center arching up. This used the weight of the skier to force the ski downward, allowing for control on cross-country runs. This design allowed for a slender ski, replacing much thicker and less flexible types. By 1868, the Telemark ski, designed by Sondre Norheim, was even more flexible and

This shows the skis used by early Sami skiers.[5]

used ash, which was strong and springy. Some 1880s designers briefly moved to hickory, but it proved too hard to work with, although later tools made working with hickory much easier. Hickory skis were even lighter and more flexible than ash. The use of hickory really took off when Scandinavian immigrants to the United States found that they had better access to the wood than their European colleagues had.[7]

In 1893, Norwegian H. M. Christiansen developed the first two-layered ski with a hickory base and a spruce or birch top. Although the woods made for excellent skis, the early glues were not reliable. With all of these improvements, there was increased demand, leading to the first ski factory, built in Switzerland by Melchior Jacober.[8]

From 1905 to 1934, inventors worked on variations of the multilayered wooden ski. A major technological change came in 1934, when Frenchman Joseph Vicky developed the first all-aluminum ski; another designer then introduced aluminum poles in 1936. From then and through the World War II era, many of the improvements to ski equipment came as outgrowths of the war industry, especially coming from inventions related to aviation. This was especially true of new types of adhesives, such as Aerolite and Redux from English engineer R. E. D. Clark. In 1945, Vought-Sikorsky, an aircraft company, began to laminate aluminum, first for their aircraft and then for skis. Aircraft engineer Howard Head made his first plasticized paper and aluminum ski in 1947. While that model did not work well, it served as a first step as he worked toward his later Head skis. The next stage, fiberglass-reinforced plastic skis, came in 1952.[9] I will provide information on the further evolution of ski design and construction through the words of our oral history informants.

NOTES

1. Natalia Klimczak, "5,000-Year-Old Rock Carving Depicting Skier in Norway Destroyed by Youths," *Ancient Origins: Reconstructing the Story of Humanity's Past*, http://www.ancient-origins.net/news-history-archaeology/5000-year-old-rock-carving-depicting-skier-norway-destroyed-youths-006380 (accessed 2/25/2018).
2. Klimczak, "5,000-Year-Old Rock Carving."
3. Miles Clark, "The Origins of Skiing," SnowBrains, https://snowbrains.com/the-origins-of-skiing-7000-years-ago/ (accessed October 8, 2020).
4. Clark, "The Origins of Skiing."
5. Clark, "The Origins of Skiing."
6. Morten Lund, Seth Masia, and Mike Brady. "A Short History of Skis," International Ski History Association, https://www.skiinghistory.org/history/short-history-skis-0 (accessed 2/25/2018).
7. Lund, Masia, and Brady, "A Short History of Skis."
8. Lund, Masia, and Brady, "A Short History of Skis."
9. Lund, Masia, and Brady, "A Short History of Skis."

This is the early mining town of Eadsville in 1910. *(Fort Caspar Museum collection)*

CHAPTER ONE

The First Skiing Community

$\mathcal{P}$RACTICALLY FROM THE TIME THE EARLIEST white settlers strapped boards to their feet to get around in the winter, skiing in Casper was a community project. Whether teaching one another to make and use rudimentary skis, carving out and maintaining trails by hand, or taking the first steps toward transforming recreational skiing into an organized activity, Casper's skiing community was in it together.

Most accounts of early skiing on Casper Mountain are anecdotal. Many stories credit miners exploring for gold, silver, copper, and asbestos with using skis and snowshoes to travel between Casper and the mountain during the winters of the 1880s and into the 1920s. Since roads were very rudimentary, winter travel was difficult at best. Some of these miners not only traveled to the mountain but also lived up there; some, all year long. Most mountain dwellers occupied cabins on scattered mining claims, but a few gathered after Charles Eads built the town of Eadsville on the southwestern side of the mountain.[1] Most of the miners gave up their claims and left by the 1910s. In the 1920s, the Lions' Club used the ghost town as a summer camp to give impoverished city children an opportunity to spend a few weeks up on the mountain for a period of fresh air and good food.[2]

Initially, mountain roads running up CY Canyon and, later on, John Hogadone's road up the western side of Garden Creek Canyon were horse trails. Hogadone was a Casper businessman and mine investor who, in the summer of 1889, recruited miners to widen his trail to accommodate wagons.[3] But winter snows made the roads and trails impassable to

Top: **Nils Fougstedt (left) and Davy Crockett at Davy's cabin, 1920s** *(Neal Forsling collection)* Bottom: **Two mountain roads: The near track is the site of the present mountain road. Hogadone's road is on the far canyon.** *(Photograph courtesy of the Denver Public Library, Western History and Genealogy Photograph collection)*

wagons, so early residents used skis and snowshoes to make the trip to Casper to pick up supplies.

Most miners eventually gave up and moved on, but a few hardy souls remained. In the 1920s, David (Davy) B. Crockett lived in a two-room cabin at his mine site in the woods, east of the current Hogadon Road. Men and women who saw the mountain as more than a place to exploit natural resources soon joined Davy. Some were visionaries who saw the rugged terrain's potential for recreational skiing, both cross-country and downhill.

Davy and his friend Nils Fougstedt, another early resident, welcomed some of these early adventurers as guests into their homes. Others built cabins in the 1920s and 1930s. Some of the homes built in this era are still standing in the twenty-first century and have become landmarks.

One of these newer arrivals was Howard Barhaug, who owned a cabin that had been built in the 1930s by Ole Fougstedt, Nils's brother. Barhaug was a recent transplant from Minnesota. Barhaug learned to ski in his native Minnesota, taught by his parents, who had been born in Norway. He used Christiana and Telemark techniques, which he taught to mountain skiers.[4]

A crucial key to developing the mountain as a recreational destination was a better road. The preferred route wound up the eastern side of the Garden Creek Canyon. In an interview, longtime mountain resident Warren Weaver described its route. "The early road up the mountain followed the present road to Asbestos Spring. At the spring, it turned west, up the Wild Oats Lane trail past the Nichols-Snedden cabin to where the streetcar is presently located, and on to Eadsville. It was a one-lane dirt road with cutoffs for passing."[5] To more clearly locate the road in modern terms, Asbestos Spring stood at the entrance to the Wild Oats Lane, now renamed O'Quinn Road. At the top end of the road, Dennis and Nancy Polk now own the Nichols-Snedden cabin.

A 1928 *Casper Tribune-Herald* article stated, "Natrona County last year spent $10,273 on the highway improvements, making

the turns wider and less dangerous and affording other conveniences of travel for motorists who annually make pilgrimages to the mountain top."[6]

Nils Fougstedt

Nils Fougstedt, originally from Kagerod, Skane, Sweden, immigrated to the United States with his brother Olaf (Ole) around 1900. Before he left Sweden, Nils earned a horticulture degree from the University of Sweden.[7] Nils and Ole spent a couple of decades in western Montana, running their own landscaping business. Census records show them in Kalispell and then in Missoula. Other records also show that Nils became an American citizen by 1910 and served in the US military in World War I.

Nils came to Casper in 1918 and poured his energy into acquiring a large homestead that, at one time, covered much of the northern face of the mountain. He owned over 450 acres on the mountain top, including land that would eventually become most of Casper Mountain's ski hills and the Hogadon Ski Area. Nils settled on the northern cliffs overlooking Casper, where he built a modest log home. He made his living building other mountain cabins and landscaping in town.

In July of 1925, the Natrona County commissioners hired him to plant trees and flowers around the new Natrona County Memorial Hospital.[8] Some of the area's sheep companies, especially the Speas Sheep Company, hired Nils to build mountain cabins for "paper homesteaders" who filed on land, lived there briefly during a summer, and gave the company grazing rights. One such cabin was at what is now Crimson Dawn.

Nils grew up skiing in Sweden and was delighted to find a place to live where he could continue his favorite outdoor activity. He used his long, wooden Swedish skis to get up the mountain when snow blocked the unpaved road, but his interest went beyond mere transportation. Fascinated by Casper Mountain's recreational potential, Nils understood that he could encourage others to take up the sport.

Early Ski Runs

In the 1920s, Nils began to develop ski runs along the front of the mountain. He cut the trees, clearing the trails, then used the logs to help build mountain cabins. One of the first runs was Thunderbolt, which began above the Nichols-Snedden cabin, ran down Wild Oats Lane trail, and then, on a trail cut by Nils, curved down the draw to the Dixie Lodge. It was no more than ten feet wide at its broadest point and varied from quite a steep drop to a gradual decline towards Dixie. It was more of a cross-country run than a downhill slope.

Over time, he added a straight vertical cut down from the heights to the eastern draw of Garden Creek. Modern residents will recognize the trail's route running from Eagle's Rest (once owned by Warren and Sara Weaver) to the bottom at Wild Oats Lane, where Donna and Dick O'Quinn have their home. Nils also spearheaded a second ski run, called Spillway, to satisfy downhill skiers who wanted more of a thrill. Starting on the ridge west of Thunderbolt, the ten-foot-wide course zigzagged down toward Garden Creek's larger, western drainage. Like Thunderbolt, it also ended near Dixie Lodge. To gain access to both Thunderbolt and Spillway, skiers would drive as far as they could and then hike the rest of the way to the top of mountain. After a long day of activity, they would then ski down to their cars. Nils did not charge a fee to use the runs because at that time, none of them had tows.

After Nils's death, the Casper Mountain Ski Club decided to add an improvement. About a few hundred yards downhill from Spillway, just to the northwest of the current Eagle's Rest, the Ski Club cut a steep, narrow slot through the pines, which was the site of an unusual tow. This was a box-like sled that an engine pulled up to the top, carrying skiers. The tow operator then reversed the motor to let the gondola down to pick up more riders. This was not the most efficient tow set-up, so a few years later, they put in a more traditional rope tow.[9] Downhill skiers still used Thunderbolt and Spillway until the late 1950s, and it still attracted cross-country skiers as late as the 2010s.

Nils befriended many Casper residents whom he inspired with his love for skiing. Among them were Cecil (Cy) and Gladys Bon, Theodore (Ted) French, Eunice and Ted Purdy, Chris and Mabel German, Ina and Byron Blake, Joe Logaway, and Jack and Jewell Cummings. Each of them, in different ways, became part of a core group that started the transition from skiing an informal, individualized sport to a more organized and commercial recreational activity on Casper Mountain. In the mid to late 1920s, this group grew to include Casper mayor Frank Cowan and his wife, Grace, as well as Stu Wagoner and Louie Keefe.[10]

In 1926, this group of skiers gets ready to head out from Nils Fougstedt's cabin. Nils is standing third from the left, without a hat. Gladys Bon is in a white hat. Cecil Bon is at the end of the line, on the right. *(Bill Bon collection)*

Nils told his Wyoming friends he had been acquainted with the famous—but doomed—Swedish polar explorer Saloman Andrée, who lost his life in 1897 while searching the Arctic for true geographic north using a hot air balloon.[11]

He gathered his friends together in November 1930 to create a club that he called the Andrée Viking Ski Club. According to an article in a 1930 *Casper Tribune-Herald* newspaper, the club's activities drew many weekend skiers, especially to increasingly popular races. The club survived Nils's sudden death from pneumonia in the Natrona County Hospital on December 9, 1930.[12] His brother Olaf (Ole) and his two sisters inherited his land and cabin.

Olaf (Ole) Fougstedt

After his brother's death in 1930, Ole moved from Kalispell, Montana, to Casper to take over Nils's holdings. Ole quickly became an integral part of both the community and the mountain skiing scene. He ran the rope tow at Nursery for many years, often assisted by Jim Forsling, Murdo Morrison, Cy Bon, and other men who came and went from the mountain. He also supported himself by cutting and selling firewood and by building cabins, including some at the foot of the Nursery Ski Run.

Ole kept diaries from 1937 to 1957 in which he recorded every person who passed by his cabin and documented the ongoing work to build up mountain skiing. He noted who was coming up and who was helping out at the runs. He also described his own work in maintaining the various hills and trails.

For instance, on February 7, 1937, he noted, "I stayed at ski track to cut trees but had to help Toad on plow, about one foot of snow. Come back, cut trees and cleared brush."[13] Ole also spent considerable time working on the old equipment that composed the Nursery ski tow. On January 14, 1937, he noted that he "finally got away to go to the ski course to look after engine." Five days later, he "helped Toad load drums for ski engine." These would presumably have been drums full of gasoline. On March 20, he found the gas tank on the engine was empty, so he brought five gallons up on the twenty-first.[14] While Ole was not the only one fixing the engine, getting it gas, or keeping it running, he was usually involved in any work at Nursery.

In other diary references, Ole documented his work to maintain the Thunderbolt run. On February 23, 1937, he wrote, "I cut grove in draw at ski track." On March 30, 1937, he said, "I worked on Thunderbolt to dark, filled in holes." On December 8, 1937, "I cut two trees on Thunderbolt, shoveled some snow." Again, on December 10, "I cut three trees on Thunderbolt," and on December 31, "I cut a tree on Thunderbolt."[15] Ole was determined to continue his brother's legacy by improving the older runs. Several oral histories reported that in the late 1930s, Nursery and Spillway continued to be the primary locations for ski races.

Ole's diaries also described his own times on skis. On February 1, 1937, he went with friends to the ski hill where his friend Toad was demonstrating new ways to turn. He noted that, "I done pretty well at it." On Jan 13, 1938, he wrote, "Arvid and I skied over to Forsling's. Real good skiing. Had a lunch there, got back 10:45."[16]

Ole especially enjoyed the children who visited with their parents. At Christmas, he gave children dollar bills as gifts. He also taught a few special children to ski. Julie York remembered that her cousin Debra Street was one of the children Ole taught to ski.[17]

Ole Fougstedt near Asbestos Spring *(Chuck Morrison collection, Casper College Western History collection)*

Cecil (Cy) Bon

One of the people interviewed for the Casper Mountain Ski History Project was Bill Bon. Bon's father, Cecil (Cy) Bon, was born in Cheyenne in 1891.[18] His parents sent him to relatives in Switzerland in 1905 to be educated, and he attended boarding schools around Europe. It was during his European sojourn that he picked up his love of skiing. Since his European relatives owned hotels, mostly in Switzerland, he had plenty of opportunities to visit places where people wintered and skied.[19]

Cy returned to Wyoming in 1912 and attended trade school in Cheyenne. He moved to Casper after World War I. He met Gladys Phillips, and after they married in the early 1920s, he introduced her to his favorite winter pastime. After Bill and his sister, Jane, were born, the couple taught the children to enjoy winter on Wyoming's slopes. Cy and Gladys were skiers throughout their adult lives, although only Cy really enjoyed downhill skiing. Gladys was happy going across the

Top: **Cy and Bill Bon skiing, 1920s. Note the long skis and only one pole.** (*Bill Bon collection*) Bottom: **Bill Bon getting the hang of the skis** (*Bill Bon collection*)

mountain, especially with the children. Cy and Gladys carried Bill around in a ruck sack when he was too small to get on skis. He guessed that they got him his first skis when he was quite small. His memory of his earliest skis was of a homemade pair made of beer keg slats held on with a stout rubber band. Later on, he got real skis with bindings.[20]

Bill Bon's memories of his early skiing experiences give us a sense of what sorts of equipment and what conditions they skied in during the 1930s. This came from Bon's oral history interview by Sam Weaver.

> Sam: We'll start with your skiing experience first. So, when did you first start skiing?
>
> Bill Bon: Oh, let's see. Probably the early '30s. 1930. My dad was interested in skiing, so I got involved in that and skied; probably started skiing when I was six or seven years old. I will say we didn't have much equipment. You could throw on a couple of beer slats and a rubber band and be all right.
>
> The early days, the slope we had at that time to my recollection was the old Nursery slope. We called it the Nursery slope. I think everybody called it that. As a matter of fact, we used to have to herringbone up that to get up and then ski back down. Then walk back up because we didn't have a tow in those early days. But that didn't really slow us down at that age. I probably started just messing around and getting cold feet and cold hands. I always had gloves that came about halfway up my wrist and then there would be a bare space and sleeves. So, some of my early experiences, I don't think I enjoyed so well. Plus, the feet would always

get cold. But as you get older, you get used to that or get better equipment. So, I probably enjoyed my skiing when I was going to high school.[21]

We know from Ole Fougstedt's diaries that Cy Bon was quite involved in setting up and improving the early ski runs. Between 1937 and 1940, there was scarcely an entry in which he did not mention Cy (whom he referred to as Si) being up on the mountain. For instance, on November 28, 1937, Ole noted that both Cy and Billie (his name for Bill) were up. Most times, Cy was bringing up a carload of young skiers, but at times, he brought others who he felt might advance the state of skiing on the mountain.

These young skiers, ready to head for the mountain, pose near Cy Bon's car. *(Bill Bon collection)*

In an entry for Tuesday, January 25, 1938, Ole noted: "Si and ski expert was up. Lionel here and was all over mountain looking for new ski jump."[22] This entry referred to an expedition, in 1939, that led to the opening of a new ski hill that skiers named Bumps-a-Daisy.

Neal and Jim Forsling

In 1923, Nils Fougstedt built the one-room cabin at what later became Crimson Dawn, on the southern side of the mountain.[23] In the summer of 1929, it became the home to

Elizabeth Paxton Ogilbee and her two daughters, Mary and Jean. Elizabeth, who went by the pen name of Neal Gallatin, was one of Casper's most significant artists. She proved to be tougher than previous homesteaders, keeping both the land and the cabin and finally receiving her homestead papers in the 1930s.

Neal married her second husband, Jim Forsling, in 1930. Throughout much of that decade, they lived at Crimson Dawn, summer and winter, and they added a second room during that time. Jim and Neal got to and from their home in the winter by skiing out to the main road.

Jim Forsling returns to Crimson Dawn *(Crimson Dawn collection)*

In 1931, Neal wrote her friend Nellie Weir in Casper about her experiences at Crimson Dawn. She recorded spending long hours alone while Jim made part of their winter income helping Ole build cabins and helping run the Nursery ski tow. In one letter, she wrote,

> Every now and then some of the skiers over on the other side of the mountain find Jim's trail over here and they follow it to see where it will go. A week ago, two young men appeared, it was terrible cold. They asked a few questions, they expected to cook their lunch outdoors. Jim and I insisted they come in and cook it inside and eat it in the cabin. They were brothers named Nunn and one of them was married to Margaret Duncan. . . . They stayed an hour and visited with us. They even left me some Scotch shortbread. . . . I did not tell you that Jim left here yesterday to go to town to get supplies. He left in the early morning. I made him promise that if he did not get up before dark he would stay on the other side because it is too dangerous to come the three miles in the dark when the snow is so deep.
>
> P.S. Jim appeared about seven with sixty pounds of grub in a pack on his back. Lots of food now.[24]

Jack and Jewell Cummings Family and the Founding of the Casper Ski Club

The Jack Cummings family also made their home on the mountain. Claude Russell (Jack) Cummings moved to Casper Mountain sometime in the late 1920s. A gregarious man, he got to know most of the mountain residents, although Nils Fougstedt seemed to be his closest friend. The two bachelors worked together and socialized with visitors and residents alike. Some of that changed when Jewell Street arrived and swept Jack off of his feet.[25]

Jewell was a native of Montana who, at seventeen, had married Lewen Bill (L. B.) Street, a cowboy who worked for her parents. Jewell and L. B. had three sons: L. B. Jr., Roy, and Jack. L. B. brought his family to Wyoming to homestead. Shortly thereafter, Jewell ended her unhappy marriage to Bill and married Jack Cummings in 1932. Bill moved to Kansas, and Jewell's boys grew up with Jack as their father.[26]

Jack and Jewell Cummings started their homestead in 1934. They acquired 640 acres that included the two drainages of Elkhorn Creek. Jack also leased state land that included the hill that became the Nursery ski run.[27] The Nursery hill was actually part of the "school section," whose sale was designed to fund local schools.

Jewell and Jack built their home in the middle of their homestead overlooking Elkhorn Canyon. Jewell's sons Roy and L. B. Street worked with Jack to cut and set corral poles. The family built tourist cabins and, by the mid-1930s, a lodge they called Wa-Wa. For decades, Wa-Wa was where visitors, including skiers, gathered for parties, dances, award ceremonies, and—perhaps most importantly—eating Jewell's famous fried chicken dinners.[28] According to Angus Morrison, Jewell also sold chili and hamburgers from the head-house of the rope tow at Nursery.[29]

The exact beginning of Nursery is a bit uncertain. A Cy Bon photograph showing a race there has a date of 1926. Julie York, granddaughter of Jack Cummings, credits her grandfather with seeing the potential of the Nursery hill, further clearing and broadening it. He recruited friends such as Ole Fougstedt, Jim Forsling, and Cy Bon to join him in the hard work of improving the open incline that the US Civilian Conservation Corps had carved out of the mountain forest. A newspaper article indicated that Cummings first called it the Andre Viking Ski Hill as an homage to Nils Fougstedt.[30] Later (and certainly by 1937), he renamed it Nursery.[31] It is unclear why he gave it that name, unless it referred to the ease of skiing on the hill. Jack and Jewell Cummings were among those early skiers who realized that skiing could become an increasingly important part of the recreational scene in Natrona County.

Another contribution of Jack's to mountain ski culture was helping to create the Casper Mountain Ski Club. After Nils died, Jack, Cy, and other friends worked with other ski aficionados to transform Nils's Andrée Viking Ski Club into the broader based Casper Mountain Ski Club. The Casper Junior Chamber of Commerce, whose members were also trying to get people interested in mountain recreation, used their clout to energize the Casper Mountain Ski Club in the 1930s.[32] Having many willing hands and minds working to promote skiing hastened the success of not only Nursery but also of the older runs, Thunderbolt and Spillway.

The founding members of the ski club included Walter (Post) McGrath, Fred Huffsmith, Stewart Wagoner, Clarence Thompson, Jack Cummings, Cy Bon, Monte Dozier, Dave Kidd, Frank Cowan, Perry Nichols, John Jourgensen, George Porter, Vince Crater, John McNulty, Don Lobdell, Nelson Van Natta, and Ole Fougstedt.

The club steadily needed to gather volunteers and to raise money. Anyone could join, and membership included use of the tow at Nursery for twenty-five cents per day. Non-members paid seventy-five cents per day to ride the tow. The *Casper Tribune-Herald* also reported that "the new Ski Club emblems have arrived and are on sale at Kistler's Western Sporting Goods Shop and the Chamber of Commerce, Post McGrath, president of the ski club announced. The emblems are of different design that those of last year and are reported to be much niftier. They will be sold at a lower price than last year."[33]

One of the first tasks taken on by the club was improving the rope tow on Nursery. As we know from Ole's diaries, there was a tow by early 1937. This first engine, a one-cylinder engine powered by gasoline, provided the power for a manila rope to pull about four or five skiers at a time from bottom to top. It was slow, but it was much better than herringboning up the slope, which skiers previously had to do at the end of each run. The ski club provided funds to pay Ole and his friends to run the tow, to provide upkeep on the rope, and to supply new engines and buy gasoline. In his diaries, Ole often reported that he had presented the club with a bill for his time or for supplies. They always paid promptly.

Top: **This race on Nursery, held in the late 1930s, was well attended by both racers and spectators.** *(Bill Bon collection)* Bottom: **In this photograph, Cy Bon is ready for the next run on Nursery in the early 1930s.** *(Bill Bon collection)*

circumstances is hazardous. The only way to pack the snow is to walk up the course sideways in skis."[34]

Some weekends, the crowd on the mountain numbered a hundred or more hardy people. That caused the club to reinvent the tow. This time, they used a Model-A engine that had much more power, and they ran a second line down the back of Nursery so people could ski there. They called that run Shaboom. Eventually, all of this was one part of a system of trails that linked to Bumps-A-Daisy, in Casper Mountain Park.

For many years, the Nursery slope continued to be the most popular skiing and sledding hill on the mountain. Many races ran from the top of the Nursery slope and ended at the bottom, mere hundreds of feet below. Over time, Nursery became so well known that ski fans, young and old, made regular treks up the unimproved, dirt mountain road to ski there. Since the road ended just past Nursery, it was also a starting point for young ski fans who would use it as the start of cross-country adventures that would take them all over the mountain top and even down Spillway and Thunderbolt. The only thing Nursery lacked was a ski jump.

John (Bud) Jourgensen credits his father, John Jourgensen, who came to Wyoming in 1914, with being an early avid skier who also trained novice skiers. He had learned to ski in his

The ski club also organized people for common tasks, such as helping pack the Nursery slope. "All skiing enthusiasts are asked to gather on the mountain top Saturday afternoon and help pack the snow. There is about a foot and a half of powdery snow on the mountain but skiing under the

native Norway. When he moved to the Scandinavian community in Chicago, he joined a ski club there and then continued to ski after moving to Casper. Jourgensen tells of how after his father returned from WWI, he got his young children skiing. He purchased skis and bindings at a cost of $4.50 for the skis and $2.50 for the bindings. The boots were heavy, square-toed, lace-up models. Clothing was whatever was warm and fairly waterproof.

Having new equipment in those days was unusual, as most people found the cost too expensive. Many people made their skis from barrel staves and tied them on with a thong to keep the skis from slipping off. Early skiers used one pole that they placed at the center of their body to steer and slow themselves down. Bud also noted that in the early 1920s, most people drove to the foot of the mountain, hiked up, and then skied back to the bottom.[35]

Theodore (Ted) French

Most of the pioneer skiers interviewed by the Casper Mountain Ski History Project mentioned Ted French. Angie Morrison, Bill Bon, Warren Weaver, and Doug French all mentioned Ted's leadership of Boy Scouts Troop #9, and all agreed that French introduced most of the future leaders of Casper skiing to the sport through Troop #9 winter expeditions onto Casper Mountain. Warren Weaver especially praised French for his skilled guidance of a whole generation of boys. Later interviewees also remembered Bill Haines Sr. as the second leader of Troop #9.

An interview by Doug French with his brother Ted revealed that their father started skiing in the 1930s because he wanted to teach Boy Scouts how to be independent in the outdoors. He and his oldest son, Bob, started the ski project

In the late 1930s, Boy Scouts Troop #9 was one of the chief ways boys in Casper got out into nature and learned to ski. Ted French is on the left, in the rear. Bill Haines is on the right. *(Weaver-Hunt collection)*

to teach the boys to make their own skis. He saw that there was very little skiing among Casper's youth and figured that if the kids had inexpensive gear, they would be more likely to get out there and learn how to ski. He bought a steamer and press to shape inexpensive hickory boards. He also purchased a jig to make the center groove. Ted reported that these were long, cross-country-style skis. The bindings were leather and canvas, which the boys also put together. Later, Ted and the Boy Scouts used the same equipment to make water skis.

Ted noted, "At that time, they would go on outings on Casper Mountain, they would have the whole mountain to themselves. The troop progressed to doing less cross-country skiing and more playing on the hills and they started to shorten the skis to allow for making quicker turns. They still made the new designs as troop projects."[36]

Ted French also had another talent—he could splice rope. This was an especially important skill when a tow rope broke. Simply knotting it together or creating a bumpy splice made the trip up a slope almost impossible when the skier hit the lump in the rope. Knotted ropes could also jump off the drive wheel, stopping the tow and stranding riders. French had a deft hand at creating a smooth transition past the former break. This endeared him to many ski aficionados, and it kept him working late many nights as he raced against the clock to finish a splice before the next day's opening or race deadline. As Doug French noted in his interview,

> My dad was one of the few people that could put in a good long splice on a rope. A long splice, when a rope breaks, is one that you could taper out as you laid it out. So, you had a smooth transition. Short splice was easy and quick to do, but a short splice left a big lump on each end of where you hooked it together. So, if you slapped a tow gripper on and then hit a short splice, it was a very rude jerk to get you going, where a long splice would let it slide through enough to get going.[37]

Doug French also noted that "being able to splice the rope, that got us a discount on ski tickets for years and years and years."[38]

1939: A Year of Progress, the Civilian Conservation Corps (CCC), and the Origins of Bumps-A-Daisy

Starting in 1933, the New Deal legislation's Civilian Conservation Corps (CCC) arrived on the mountain. The CCC brought young men from all over the United States to work in western local, state, and national forests. Workers from the Casper CCC camp

Warren and Wayne Weaver with their ski equipment, late 1930s. Both learned to ski in Troop #9. *(Weaver-Hunt collection)*

planted trees, cut fire breaks, and helped develop and maintain ski and other recreational areas on the mountain.[39] Improvements on the the Nursery slope began when the CCC decided to widen it as one of their fire breaks. Because Jack Cummings was leasing the land from the state at that time, he used the widening efforts to improve his ski slope and attract more skiers.

A decade of dreaming about expanding the mountain runs and trails came to fruition in 1939. The increase in the number of skiers was fueled by new marketing, especially that done by the Casper Mountain Ski Club and the Casper Junior Chamber of Commerce. The Civilian Conservation Corps also helped build cross-country trails, including two that were part of the Bumps-a-Daisy complex.

In 1939, the CCC, working with the Casper Mountain Ski Club and the chamber of commerce, began clearing land and building a three-part ski area in Casper Mountain Park. These were part of the Bumps-a-Daisy complex. The *Casper Tribune-Herald* documented the course in an article in 1939.

> The CCC is now busy completing units of the winter sport development jointly sponsored by the Casper Mountain Ski Club and the Casper Junior Chamber of Commerce, the job of constructing the new slalom course is all but finished. It is 800 feet long and will be served by the new No. 2 tow. No. 1 continues in service at the Nursery slope. It was designed for practice by advanced skiers and for slalom competition, the new course is situated about three-eighths of a mile north and east of the Lions' camp, just off the highway.
>
> Further work by the CCC under the direction of the national park service superintendent C. D. Marshal, will include construction of a 30-meter ski jump and down-mountain trail on either side of the slalom, so that, all three courses will be served by the new tow. A shelter will be built, for the tow motor and ultimately there will be a shelter for skiers at the bottom of the runs.

> The slalom course will easily be one of best in the entire mountain region where skiing is active, and the new No. 2 tow built by the mountain ski club, the junior chamber and the CCC provides devotees on Casper mountain with facilities available at few other winter sports areas. Sun Valley, Idaho is one of these few.
>
> The mountain road will be kept open to both the new and old ski areas by the county highway department announced the county commissioners who did such a fine job of clearing the road last year to the acclaim of the large number of skiers who took advantage of it.
>
> Plans for a series of competitive events this winter, after good snow surface conditions are realized have been prepared. The Casper Mountain Ski Club shortly will open its 1939–40 membership campaign.[40]

The Mystery of the Nursery Ski Jump

Ted French was involved in a short-lived milestone in 1939. Many skiers had wanted a ski jump somewhere on one of the existing runs. The ski club was working on the one at Bumps-A-Daisy, but it was slow in coming. One weekend as people arrived at Nursery, they found a modestly sized ski jump constructed on one side of the slope. Angry skiers quickly tore down the jump, claiming that jumpers would be a danger to other skiers. The mystery of the ski jump was solved when French sent a letter to the editor of the *Casper Times*. He admitted to helping to build the jump, but he argued that many ski club members supported it and that only a few hotheads had banded together to destroy the new amenity. French wrote,

> If the lack of knowledge on the part of seven or eight people out of membership of two or three hundred, makes a mystery out of an act, then there is a mystery, but such was not intended. A practice jump was built on a practice slope in such a way and

Skiers walk up the Casper Mountain road in the ruts from the last car to get through in 1926. *(Bill Bon collection)*

place as not to interfere with others enjoying the same slope. The substantial improvement did not take a whole day and was built Tuesday by two members of the club, whose time and materials were NOT charged to the club. It was too bad that the structure was destroyed by a few before the rest of the members had a chance to decide whether they would enjoy it or not. But such is life—a few decide for the many. Casper lost the tournament this year because of the lack of such a structure, because the CCC did not do it. Why wait for others to do things when they can be done by ourselves in such a short time—two men in less than one day. If the few do not get impatient another mystery might appear on the other hill as was originally planned.[41]

A Growing Reputation

People from other areas of the state were also increasingly attracted to Casper Mountain. In 1939, Agnes Wright Spring, a writer for the *Wyoming Stockman-Farmer* newspaper, wrote an article about the best ski areas in Wyoming. She highlighted other ski hills, including the run west of Laramie, up in the Snowy Range. This was an area that many interviewees who had attended the University of Wyoming remembered skiing at as they practiced for the university ski team. Spring then devoted much of her article to the growing recreational skiing and racing opportunities at Nursery. In addition, a *Casper Tribune-Herald* report by Frances Seely Webb in the fall of 1939 documented the efforts of the Casper Junior Chamber of Commerce and the Casper Mountain Ski Club to add lights to Nursery. The article noted that as soon as the lights came on line and there was enough snow, night skiing would commence.[42] The chamber of commerce argued that it was a chance to give hard-working businessmen a chance to ski on winter nights, so they turned on the lights midweek to lure them up.

Getting Up the Mountain

Because the mountain road was not paved until 1940, getting to the skiing area had not improved much since the early days. In the early 1920s, Ole recorded that his friend Toad ran a plow to apparently open the road to Nursery. He did not say if it was a government plow or one owned by a mountain resident. The one improvement was that the county plowed more often. But when the snow bucketed down and the wind howled, the trip could be difficult and sometimes dangerous. A number of the oral history interviewees described their experiences on the mountain road.

Sam Weaver, during his interview of Doug French, shared one of Warren Weaver's stories about traveling up Casper Mountain with Ted French. According to the account, French had a big touring car that pulled a trailer. He piled all of the equipment and some of the Boy Scouts into the trailer and fit the rest into the touring car. Doug French described an old truck that his dad, Ted, used to bring the scouts up. Scouts and gear were all crowded into the truck. He also mentioned that since it was so hard to put on tire chains, most drivers would do almost anything to avoid having to stop to chain up.[43]

As a child, around 1937 or 1938, Marge Stuckenhoff often went up to ski, driving with Howard Barhaug. He took her up because his own children were not interested in skiing. His Model T touring car did not have windows on the sides.

Marge clearly remembered the cold trips.[44] Virtually every interviewee had some variation on this same story. Many also talked about how far they had to walk to even get to the slopes.

It says a lot about the resilience of Casper skiers that they could hike up the mountain, pack the slopes, and then ski the rest of the day. Many then spent the night at Ole's cabin or at other "loaner" cabins. That gave them time to recover and then go on day (and even night) cross-country adventures. Many described gliding through mountain meadows and zooming down canyons. They did not require properly groomed trails, but they frequently made their own. But, by the end of the 1930s, Casper's skiing community, with the help of the federal government, had built the foundations of a thriving, organized recreational ski facility on the mountain.

As the decade of the 1930s came to an end, Casper's skiers, young and old, viewed the future of recreation on the mountain with considerable hope and enthusiasm. Little did the young generation know that they would shortly have to postpone their dreams to go off and fight a world war.

NOTES

1. Rebecca A. Hunt, *Natrona County: People, Place, and Time* (Virginia Beach, VA: The Donning Company Publishers, 2011), 68.
2. "Casper Mountain Grows in Popularity as Playground," *The Casper Tribune-Herald*, February 6, 1927, 7.
3. Hunt, *Natrona County*, 60.
4. Marge Stuckenhoff, Casper Mountain Ski History Project, oral history interview by Sam Weaver, September 26, 2016, 2.
5. Warren (Buck) Weaver, interview by MaryAnn Hoff, n.d.
6. "Recreational Advantages of Casper Are Varied," *The Casper Tribune-Herald*, February 19, 1928, 20.
7. "Nils Fougstedt Taken by Death," *Casper Herald Tribune*, December 1930, 19.
8. Rebecca A. Hunt, *Wyoming Medical Center: A Centennial History* (Virginia Beach, VA: The Donning Company Publishers, 2010), 33.
9. Weaver, interview.
10. Bill Bon, Casper Mountain Ski History Project, oral history interview by Sam Weaver, November 10, 2013, 5.
11. Wilbur Cross and Thorleif Hellbom, "Solomon August Andrée – Sweden: The First Attempt of a Flight to the North Pole," http://www.aviation-history.com/airmen/andree.htm (accessed April 5, 2021).

12. Nils Fougstedt obituary, *Casper Tribune-Herald*, December 1930.
13. One thing to note: Ole called people by their first or last names—rarely by both. Toad, Mrs. Toad, and Little Toad frequently turned up in the diaries between 1937 and 1939 when they apparently left Casper. They seem to have lived on the mountain for some of that time, and then in town. Toad was a frequent assistant to Ole in his ski endeavors, as well as in his cabin building, tree felling, and road grading.
14. Ole Fougstedt, diary, 1937.
15. Fougstedt, diary, 1937.
16. Ole Fougstedt, diaries for 1937–38. Arvid was another of Ole's frequent helpers.
17. Julie York, "Family Reminiscences," e-mail to the author, February 27, 2019.
18. Bon, interview, 4.
19. Bon, interview, 5.
20. Bon, interview, 7.
21. Bon, interview, 1.
22. Ole Fougstedt, diary, January 25, 1938.
23. Neal Forsling, caption on photograph of Nils Fougstedt and Dave Crockett, 1929.
24. Neal Forsling, letter to Nellie Weir, winter, 1931.
25. York, "Family Reminiscences."
26. York, "Family Reminiscences."
27. York, "Family Reminiscences."
28. York, "Family Reminiscences."
29. Angus Morrison, Casper Mountain Ski History Project, oral history interview by Sam Weaver, April 7, 2009, 9.
30. Fougstedt obituary.
31. In his 1937 diary, Ole Fougstedt talked about working at the Nursery slope.
32. "New Slalom Course on Casper Mountain Will Relieve Congestion," *Casper Tribune-Herald*, 1939.
33. "New Slalom Course," *Casper Tribune-Herald*, 1939.
34. "New Slalom Course," *Casper Tribune-Herald*, 1939.
35. Weaver, interview.
36. Doug French, e-mail to Jackie Ellis, Rebecca Hunt collection, August 11, 2009.
37. Doug French, Casper Mountain Ski History Project, oral history interview by Sam Weaver and Sean Ellis, August 8, 2009, 7.
38. French, interview, 6.
39. "New Slalom Course," *Casper Tribune-Herald*, 1939.
40. "New Slalom Course," *Casper Tribune-Herald*, 1939.
41. T. R. (Ted) French, letter to the editor, *Casper Times*, 1939.
42. Frances Seely Webb, *Casper Tribune-Herald*, 1939.
43. French, interview, 7.
44. Stuckenhoff, interview, 1.

162
Road down Casper Mountain
near "Dixie Lodge"

CHAPTER TWO

Organizing

❄ ❄ ❄

This is the Casper Mountain road in early 1940, just before Natrona County paved it. Note that the cabin in the valley is Dixie Lodge, one of the after-ski spots for those skiing on Miner, Spillway, and Thunderbolt. *(Phil Cole collection)*

*R*OB ROBERTSON, DWIGHT OSBORN, DICK PERKINS, and Marge Stuckenhoff were skiing Nursery when they got word of the attack on Pearl Harbor on December 7, 1941.[1] As America went to war, Robertson, Osborn, Perkins, and most of the other men in Casper prepared to volunteer or to get their notice from the draft board. Many women prepared to sign up to work in the war industry.[2]

A few of Casper's young skiers became part of the legendary Tenth Mountain Division. This unit trained at Camp Hale, near Leadville, Colorado. Most of its recruits were members of elite ski teams drawn from Ivy League schools. But the unit also included men who had grown up in the West. These men had—like many of Casper's skiers—learned to ski in areas like Jackson, Wyoming, Sun Valley, Idaho, and in Montana. Some also had experience at mountaineering. One Casper skier who joined the 10th Mountain Division was Wayne Weaver, who had learned to ski in Ted French's Boy Scouts Troop #9.[3]

This map created by Sam Weaver shows Nursery, Spillway, Thunderbolt, Miner, Bumps-A-Daisy, and—after 1958—Hogadon. *(Laurie Weaver collection)*

As it disrupted individual lives, the war also forced the ski community to suspend most of its plans for developing the area's facilities. But Casper's winter recreational life continued nevertheless. During World War II, some residents remained on the mountain. Ole Fougstedt, Jim Forsling, and Neal Forsling wintered over during the winter of 1942. Others drove up to ski whenever they had a chance. As the war progressed, young men returning on leave spent part of their time on the slopes. Angie Morrison remembered that when he was on leave, he and his friends often spent more time on the mountain than in town with their families. He felt his mother may have been a bit grumpy with him because of his neglect. At one point, he had a ten-day leave and spent ten days skiing with friends, including Alan Coates, Hal Engstrom, and Bruce Sneddon.[4]

But not all ski stories were lighthearted. On March 4, 1942, Jim Forsling became a victim of the winter weather. On March 3, he skied down to where he had his truck parked. He then drove to Casper to buy groceries. On his return, he stopped off at Ole Fougstedt's cabin to warm up and have a few drinks before he started the long cross-country trip to Crimson Dawn. Apparently, a storm came up as he was leaving Ole's cabin. The old mountaineer had urged him to stay through the worst of it, but Jim did not want his wife, Neal, to worry. While skiing home, the weather got even worse and he sat down to rest, eventually dropping off into a cold-induced sleep.

On March 8, Ole got a note from Neal telling him that Jim had never arrived home. Recovery teams hurried to the mountain. A group of Boy Scouts from Ted French's Troop #9 were the first to find Jim, on the far end of Bear Trap. He had frozen to death. One young man went ahead to Crimson Dawn and let Neal know they were taking the body to town. The rest put Jim on a rescue sled and took him to the road. There was a funeral a few days later, and when spring came, Neal had him buried in a cemetery she created on the Red Butte at Crimson Dawn.[5]

Accounts vary about how much Nursery was open during the war. In the years following America's entry into World War II, most of the skiers between the ages of eighteen and fifty went off to war. But younger and older folks still turned up to ski. Ole Fougstedt kept the best records, and they showed that as early as January of 1942, there were steady numbers of weekend visitors at the slope. Until 1944 or 1945, Ole was busy running the Nursery tow whenever the roads were open enough to get up. Since the Casper Mountain Ski Club used the money from tow tickets to keep things running, the few dollars earned each week paid Ole's wages and for gas, repair parts, and new rope.[6]

Ole also noted that between January and May 1942, the ski club once again tried to have night skiing. The problem was that the wind blew so much—and the temperature was so consistently cold—that the lights rarely worked beyond one use. The winter of 1942 was unusually snowy well into May. That allowed for a longer ski season but also meant more days of blocked roads. According to Ole, a good day of driving the mountain road was one when one did not have to chain up or dig out.[7]

By 1943, Ole recorded that many visitors were soldiers, especially officers from the Casper Army Air Base. Business was good for the Cummingses at Wa-Wa, as that became a favorite stop for these visitors.[8] Ole frequently reported that the US Army was using the mountain for winter training, on horses, skis, and snowshoes. They also paid Jewell Cummings to cook special dinners at Wa-Wa. The soldiers often stopped at Ole's house. He helped them get unstuck from the blown-in road, and they brought him food, beer, and whiskey as a reward. One base chaplain, Reverend Mingus, seemed to have taken Ole on as his special project, bringing up food and newspapers and keeping him company.[9]

In 1943, the ski area was mostly open only on Sundays, probably because of gas rationing. At one point in March of 1943, Ole reported counting his gas ration coupons to see if he had enough to buy gas for the ski club to run the tow at Nursery. One side problem of being open only one day per week was that young skiers would sneak up, break into the tow shack, and run the engine. More than once, Ole caught them at it. Another thing Ole reported was the struggle to keep the rope serviceable. There were occasional references to guys coming up and having to splice the rope before anyone could use the tow. They also had to heat up the engine with a blowtorch in order to thaw the water in the radiator before the engine would start.[10]

After World War II and as people returned from the war, they once again rediscovered the joys of civilian life. That included starting and raising families, making a living, and devoting time to leisure activities. One of those was skiing. Bob Kidd, an oral history interviewee and noted ski instructor, remembered that "the mountain and skiing was a gathering place for veterans of World War II and [the] Korean Conflict, a generation that worked and played together. The races were big and super competitive, and the volume of skiers outgrew the rope tow runs."[11]

Slopes, rope tows, and hamburger shacks that suited the prewar skier soon proved to be inadequate for the rapidly growing and changing postwar ski crowd. The old rope tows, once a boon to the skiers of the 1930s, were not really suited to the growing crowds of family skiers. Another problem was the lack of a place to warm up. The previous generation had simply kept warm by being active or sitting in a car. It was tougher for families, especially those with young children. Tom Stroock remembered it this way. "When your wife came up, she would stay in there, and you opened a bottle of rum, which we had from Havana, and guzzled that down with quinine water and ate hamburgers, which weren't the best. We took our kids up to Nursery when they were little. Margie loved to ski but would get cold and go back to the car."[12]

The group of dedicated enthusiasts in the Casper Mountain Ski Association responded to some of the demands and set out to develop new slopes and cross-country trails and to organize races and other events. At first, that did not include such amenities as warming huts, bathrooms, or improved tows. That came with the development of Hogadon, beginning in 1958. The main focus was to find some more challenging terrain. That allowed Nursery to become a family slope, as the advanced skiers returned to the area around Spillway and Thunderbolt.

Miner Run

In 1946, Casper Mountain Ski Club members worked over the spring and summer of 1946 to clear trees to carve out a 100-foot-wide, 350-foot-long run that became the newest intermediate slope on the mountain. Located just up the hill from Spillway, it was on land they had purchased from Ole Fougstedt, who had inherited it from his brother Nils. It

Miner Run sign *(Weaver-Hunt collection)*

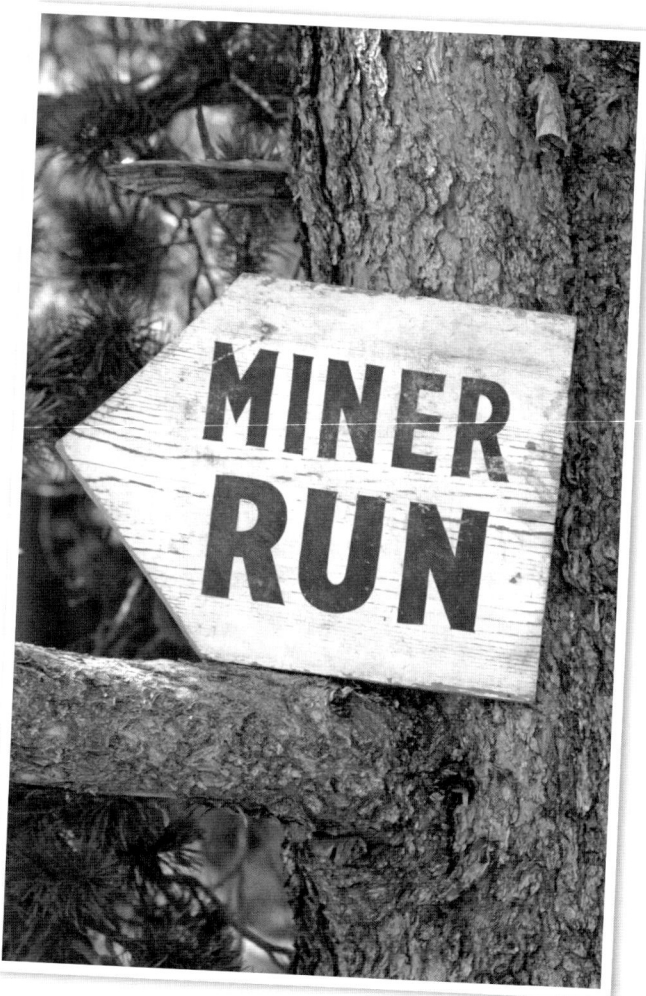

Left: **Ski-race day at Miner Run, 1955** *(Fred Walters collection)* Top right: **Miner tow shack. Left to right: Angus Morrison, Bill Haines, Shirley Haines, Barry Horn, Pat Haines, and Chuck Morrison.** *(Glenn Bochmann collection)* Bottom right: **Bill Haines racing on Miner** *(Glenn Bochmann collection)*

ended in the main drainage of the western branch of the Garden Creek below.[13] The group named the new run after Lee Miner, a young Casper skier who died in World War II. Miner had skied in Casper and then was a member of the University of Wyoming team. He had also been an active promoter of skiing on the mountain.[14]

Miner and Spillway became the go-to hills for ski races, large and small. Once a year, the Casper Mountain Ski Club organized the City Race. The date was in late winter or early spring, usually in March, when there was the best snow on the mountain. The name spoke to the fact that it was open to all comers. Each year's racing committee ran the grand

slalom on Miner because its straight drop and width made it perfect for that kind of a race. Spillway hosted the downhill because its zigzag design—with narrow and tight turns—made it an exciting and fast race.[15]

During the ski history interviews, many informants described Spillway. Bill Ladd said, "Downhill from Miner Run, it was cut from the hillside by Nils Fougstedt in the 1920s. It was a zigzag run through the trees. Spillway was kind of a corkscrew down through the mountain. Or down through the hill next to Miner. We would also hold the slalom races on Miner, and the downhill race was always on Spillway."[16]

Like all slopes at the time, the tow was made by the skiers themselves. Rob Robertson, whose family ran the Dodge dealership in town, supplied more than one truck engine for the mountain slopes. Frank (Pinky) Ellis reported that "Rob did the same thing when Miner was cut and installed. He donated a [new] engine to that. That was a sizable gift at that time. I imagine those engines probably cost a thousand bucks, maybe not that much."[17] But sometimes, Robertson did not have access to a spare engine.

Angie Morrison related a story about a mishap at the Miner tow. The day before a big race, the engine burned up, taking the tow shack with it. Thad Walker scoured the town and found out that Duane Ludden's father had a Dodge Power Wagon engine. The guys hauled it up, and on Friday night, Don Burgess organized skiers to cut any trees that made the course hazardous and to get the engine working to power the tow. They then set up the flags and gates and had the course all ready for the Saturday and Sunday races.[18]

Rope tows were still a problematic way to get back up a slope, and even more so on a very steep incline. It was hard to get a good grip, and the rope wore out many pairs of gloves.[19] Almost all of the pioneer skiers interviewed talked about the frustrations and hazards of the tows. Some purchased metal tow grippers. The skier grabbed the rope with the gripper and held on for dear life.

Top: Ann Otteson and Barry Horn after they won the Alpine race at Two Ocean Mountain at the top of Togwotee Pass. Note the tow grip on his belt. *(Glenn Bochmann collection)*
Bottom: Riding the Miner and Spillway rope tow *(Photograph by Glenn Bochmann)*

It was also easy to get clothing caught in the rope. Marge Stuckenoff remembered that Thad Walker went through the top of the lift at Miner. His clothing got caught in the drive wheel and the person running the tow had to rescue him. Marge noted that Thad's friends felt he was accident prone, so they were not surprised.[20] The larger lesson is that the rope tows were not just inappropriate but dangerous to the changing character of the skiing population, especially kids.

Brookside Inn stood on the edge of the mountain road above Garden Creek.

Once skiers got to the bottom of the slopes, they could take the rope tow back up or continue down the creek, eventually connecting to Thunderbolt and ending up at Dixie Lodge. Friends would drive to Dixie, pick up a load of skiers, and take them back up to Nursery to start over.

For those wanting to rest after the run, the Dixie Lodge offered a warm fire, hot drinks, and a few food choices, including hamburgers. Just uphill from the Dixie Lodge, on the paved road, was also a bar and restaurant called Brookside. Clarence and Martha Littlefield, who also owned the cabins at Brookside on Garden Creek, originally opened the restaurant, which had a larger food selection. By the 1940s, they had turned it over to the Clarks.

Dixie, Brookside, and the Cummingses' Wa-Wa Lodge at the top of the mountain all took turns hosting awards ceremonies after races.

Club plans also called for a lodge at the bottom of Miner. However, that proved to be hard to do.[21] Fortunately, one of

Wa-Wa après ski, 1950s

the club's committee members had an idea. Buck Weaver had purchased some land on the point below the top of Miner Run, and in 1946, he began building a round house made of vertically set logs. Many skiers helped build the cabin, and it soon became the semiofficial warming hut and clubhouse

Top left: **Building Eagle's Rest, Buck Weaver's place (Miner and Spillway lodge)** *(Weaver-Hunt collection)* Top right: **Relaxing at Weaver's place. Howie Bronsdon is on the left, Dub Darnell is in the center, and Buck is on the right. Buck is wearing the Casper Mountain Ski Club sweater.** *(Weaver-Hunt collection)* Right: **The ski parking lot at Buck's cabin after a City Race** *(Glenn Bochmann collection)* Bottom: **Racers gather after a City Race circa 1950. Rear from the left, red jacket: Fred Walters; man in suit: Lou Kistler; front row, third from the left: Barry Horn, Susan Nichols, Bill Haines, and Pat Haines (sister).** *(Glenn Bochmann collection)*

Left: The jagged line through the trees is Spillway as it looked in 2020. Buck Weaver's house is in the lower-right corner of the photograph. *(Weaver-Hunt collection)*

Right: Skiing down Spillway *(Glenn Bochmann collection)*

for Miner, Spillway, and Thunderbolt skiers. Fred Walters remembered it as the starting point for skiers making runs on all three nearby ski trails.

Glenn Bochmann, who had grown up in the ski community, returned from the military in 1955 and quickly rejoined the Casper Mountain Ski Club. In a 2011 interview, he remembered that the active members included Pat Haines, her brother Bill, and most of the other "pioneers" of skiing. He also described a typical skiing day on the mountain. A good day was one during which he did not have to chain up to reach the top or get stuck and have to hike most of the way. Once up, people could park in the lot at Nursery, make a few runs, and then go cross-country to Miner and Spillway. Many people parked at Asbestos Spring and hiked up the old road. They then hiked up the hill toward Buck's house and on to the two ski runs.[22]

In his 2019 interview, Mike Huber, another member, gave a description of Miner and Spillway.

You'd go down to the bottom, but they had a rope tow out. Then when you'd come back, you'd come down that road to come back. You know where Buck Weaver's round house is? Miner is probably, oh, I'd guess about four hundred yards or so to what I would call the west. It was sort of a straight shot down. It was just cut out. There was actually a lift line right beside it. Then, in between Miner and Buck's house, was what was called Spillway. Miner was more just a straight downhill, more kind of the expert run. And Spillway was kind of a zig-zag thing down through there. Even when I was in high school and junior high and first started going up there, I remember skiing that with Sam and with some of the other ski patrol people. Howie and all that bunch. Miner was starting to get grown in with little pine trees. Going down there, you can put your imagination to work. But the last time that I was in there, which was probably about seven years or so ago, Miner was really grown in. But Spillway hadn't ever really grown in that much.[23]

Getting There

Transportation was still a challenge in the postwar period. Several interviewees recalled that in the late 1930s or early 1940s, the Casper Mountain Ski Club had acquired six old school busses to take youngsters up the mountain. The long buses held sixty children; the shorter ones held about twenty. The young skiers had to make reservations and pay to ski, but the ride was free. The club members took turns driving. They met the kids in the morning at the armory at Durbin and Fifteenth Streets, filled the bus with youngsters and their equipment, and started up the hill. Charlie Peak remembered the road and the buses from the late 1940s in this 2016 ski history interview with Sam Weaver.

> Weaver: How were the roads coming up in those days? Were they plowed?
>
> Peak: You know, I don't believe they were steadily plowed. They were pretty rough. I can remember riding up in the old yellow bus one day with Dad driving. We got on the face there below—we got above the hard switchback and below the lookout point on that face there, and just couldn't go any further. And he had it chained up and it just ground to a halt. So, old George got everybody off the bus and he walked up the road. Everybody'd walk up behind him and they packed the trail up and back down. Then back up a little bit and hit those trails. I think he had to do that a couple times to get up there, get around the corner where the wind had blown it off.
>
> I do remember that early road, that old bus, when he'd hit those switchbacks, he'd have to do a three-point turnaround on them because that bus couldn't make the switchback. He'd have to back it up.
>
> Weaver: That's interesting. That was just a single-lane road in those days, wasn't it?
>
> Peak: Pretty much was, yeah.
>
> Weaver: With a few turnouts that let someone go by.
>
> Peak: Of course, they had—by the time I got my driver's license, they had rebuilt it, you know; it was a half-decent road at that time.
>
> Weaver: Right.
>
> Peak: But, yeah, the first road was pretty treacherous.
>
> Weaver: Then how far could you make it with the bus before you would park and go onto the ski area?
>
> Peak: Oh, he'd make it right to Nursery.
>
> Weaver: Okay. Was that kinda the end of the road in those days?
>
> Peak: Well, Bumps-a-Daisy was.[24]

Glenn Bochmann remembered that beginning in 1955, he was one of the drivers. Others included Rob Robertson, George Peak, and Don Burgess.[25] The busses ran from the 1940s and most of the 1950s. The tow ticket sales that went with the ride were a source of much of the ski club's income. In 1959, after Hogadon opened and then management passed

These children are being driven to ski in one of the Casper Mountain Ski Club busses. *(Glenn Bochmann collection)*

Top: Pushing the bus just to ski: Sometimes, the heavy snows and lack of plowing required skiers to walk partway up. In this case, the kids got off the bus and pushed it through the deep snow. Bob Kidd, the youngster in the foreground, was too young to help push. *(Photographs by Bob Kidd)* Right: Marvin Bishop and a friend get to the end of the travelable part of the Casper Mountain road. The only option was walking the rest of the way up to ski. *(Susan Bishop collection)*

to Ed Boland, the club discontinued the bus service because it did not make a profit.[26] Later on, the school district took over the provision of transportation.[27]

The increase in interest in winter sports inspired local businesspeople, the chamber of commerce, and county officials to consider ways to enhance the role that skiing might play in economic development. In 1940, the state of the mountain road caused this group of local movers and shakers to approach the county commission about paving the mountain road. The county agreed to take on the task of raising money.

But the catch was that they had to bring the Wyoming Highway Department on board. A contingent of local officials drove to Cheyenne, met with Governor Nels Smith, and got him to agree to commit state resources to paving the Casper Mountain road. The county matched the state's help with $10,000. Work began in the summer of 1940.[28] By the time of the winter ski season, the new paved road made it easier to reach the ski hills, although winter weather was still the major obstacle to mountain access. And, during the war, the road was often not plowed.

Improving Bumps-a-Daisy

Bumps-a-Daisy was originally developed by mountain residents and the Civilian Conservation Corps in the 1930s. According to Charlie Peak, a ski project interviewee and son of George Peak, by the time the new generation came along, they gave it a nickname. They called it Bumpsy.[29] Now, Bumps-a-Daisy needed more trails and a better ski jump.

Bumps-a-Daisy originally had a few trails that ran across the hillside, near the road. In the 1950s, they expanded the trails to the top of the hill, on a point that looked out over the plains to the north. Later, these runs would become part of the modern cross-country trail system.

This skier is racing down the trail at the improved Bumps-A-Daisy ski area. *(Glenn Bochmann collection)*

Glenn Bochmann remembered that the new jump was engineered by George Peak, who grew up in Montana. Peak was an engineer who had been in the US Navy's Seabees in the Pacific in World War II. He came to Casper to work for the Soil Conservation Service, pioneering snow surveys as the state director.[30]

When it came time to design a new jump, George and his team crafted the frame from lodgepole pines. The skiers shoveled snow onto the ramp when needed, which allowed people to glide down the ramp at a very high rate of speed. While the downhill and cross-country sections were fairly easy going, the jump was fast and dangerous to all but the hardiest and most expert skiers.

Fred Walters had a particularly complete description of the design and construction of the jump. When Fred was in high school, he and his friends helped George Peak build, repair, and expand the ski jump at Bumps-a-Daisy.

> One of our classmates, Dick Schirk, he had graduated and was becoming an engineering student at Casper College. And he and George Peak and some other folks designed what the hill should look like. So, part of the hill was cut with a bulldozer, and the other part we had to cut trees down, hand carry them through the forest, and then build that jump. Towards the end, we were probably in one to two feet of snow putting it together. That happened, I think, during my sophomore year in high school.[31]

George Peak's son, Charlie Peak, added to the picture in his ski history project interview.

> Charlie Peak: I think Bumpsy was everybody's favorite. They liked to be over there quite a bit. I think that the road situation kind of dictated whether we could get over there or not. I can't tell you when it was, but Dad built a jump over on Bumpsy. There was kind of a fire break on

Bumps-a-Daisy— around here and then to the north of that, there was a little fire break that paralleled it. Old George went in there— and he had a lot of help. All the local group, your dad was probably in on that. They built it up out of little lodgepoles, you know. Framed it all and then decked it with the lodgepole . . . . He was the engineer. He was the head push behind it, I know that. They had said that the push behind that was that in those days, you had Alpine, Nordic, and jumping as the three phases of skiing. And the people coming out of Casper didn't have the jumping because we didn't have a jump. That was kind of the push to build—that is the story I've gotten over the years.

I know I went off of it one time, just after the first year they set it up. I was following some older boys around and they jumped off and I thought, what the heck? I went off it pretty slow and didn't make it over the knoll on the end and cratered on there. My knee hit myself in the face. So, I was standing down the line, the rope tow line, waiting to grab hold of the rope when my dad skied up and said, "My god, what happened to you?" I said, "Well, I tried to jump." So, he thought about it a little bit, and then he went over there and he extended the lip of the jump out. He extended it out I think about eight feet. So, we could just— no jumping to it, just ride off of it.

Then when we'd start jumping, we were landing clear down at the bottom of it. So, then he moved it back. It had two feet of snow on top of the lip. Well, he left the wood part there and just cut the snow off. So, then we were cruising off the snow, and you had to jump a little bit to make it over the end. Mind you, I was probably eight years old.

It was every week we were going jumping; it was a big deal for us, that long winter.

Me and Les and Bill Galbraith that was jumping with us, the three of us were there every weekend on Dad's modified jump. Then he cut the whole thing away and tore the deck off that he'd built. And we were jumping. Even in high school, after they built Hogadon and everybody abandoned that end of the mountain, I used to drive up there and hike up, sidestep up, packing, and jump two or three times up there all by myself. Quit because it was getting dark.[32]

Here is another Charlie Peak memory:

Sam Weaver: Did they have that as part of the racing program in those days, where they would do the slaloms?

Peak: No, I don't think there was competition on that jump. Like I say, I was pretty young. Somebody older— I could ask— Steve Campbell's still alive, my sister's husband. He's still alive and got good recollections of the mountain. I'll ask him if there was ever any— get back to you on that one.

Weaver: Going back to coming up here. So, you would come up and spend the day. Was there any place to really warm up other than just that little shack? And was that at the top of Nursery? Or did they have one at Bumps-a-Daisy?

Peak: Yeah, there was. I remember there was a small shack they finally put down on Bumps-a-Daisy. I think it was like the last year or maybe two years before they built Hogadon. But it was just a little tiny thing. They had a wood heater in it. I remember you had to build a fire to warm it up.

Weaver: Yeah, that jump has pretty good history. That's the best information we've gotten on that. That's good.

Peak: I'll be interested to see some of that. I thought I was the last one to jump off of it because I jumped it in '65. I was up there jumping on it. Then I quit. And I saw a few years later, it was in pretty bad shape. Somebody'd stolen a bunch of the logs off it, probably for firewood or whatever. But I talked to Kent Doing. And apparently him and Mike Huber were up there jumping it when they were in high school. They were three or four years behind me. So obviously I wasn't the last one.

I remember it being in pretty rough shape. In fact, I was thinking that Bob Adams probably tore it down because it was then in the Parks and it became kind of a hazard. I remember stories of people breaking their leg going over it. And I think it kind of got to the point of, he says, "We've got to get rid of this thing. It's become a public nuisance."

Weaver: I think that by the time I got into high school, it was gone by then.

There was still the pro trap for where the outrun made the transition from the logs to the ground. They pushed up dirt against the ramp where that little jump of dirt is still here right now. I was up there a couple years ago.[33]

In his interview with the ski history project members, Glenn Bochmann stated that he refused to use the jump. He said that it was popular with young daredevil skiers, but many of the interviewees remembered harrowing experiences there. Some recorded near misses with broken bones, and others noted sprains and bruises from their attempts to make the run.[34]

There is one other memory of Bumps-a-Daisy, from Sam Weaver, that bridges the end of that era and the beginning of the Hogadon era.

I think we were the only one that had a portable rope tow that I've ever seen. We had this portable rope tow. We have a picture of it. We used that [tow] initially at Bumps-a-Daisy before we put a permanent tow there. That was the third ski area on the mountain, which came later. We also took it over to where Hogadon is today, but we didn't know it was going to be Hogadon. We just accidentally pulled it over there behind a Tucker snowcat one day and found this wide-open area where Boomerang is, fairly wide open. We set it up there and skied probably five years before Hogadon was in existence.[35]

Frank (Pinky) Ellis remembered how it got a tow line. "After the war, sometime between 1945 and 1947, Rob Robertson donated a new Chrysler engine to run a tow at Bumps-a-Daisy. They used a truck to haul it up the hill as far as they could, and then a bunch of guys pulled it up the

The Casper Mountain Ski Club's president, Bill Ladd, demonstrates the new portable Bumps-a-Daisy tow in 1952. *(Casper Tribune Herald; photograph by Mike Leon)*

This view of the Hogadon area—looking across the Garden Creek canyon—was taken before the ski area existed. *(Phil Cole collection)*

rest of the way."[36] They also acquired a portable tow that they used on parts of this run. It could also be moved to other areas that needed a temporary lift.[37]

After Hogadon opened, the Bumps-a-Daisy area was abandoned and began to grow over. The ski jump fell into ruin and was partly torn down by county parks director Bob Adams and his crew. But in a 2019 ski history oral interview, Jim Miller noted that some of his Nordic skiers still tried to build up and then jump off of the old ski jump. He said, "And kids every year, it doesn't matter what year, kids will find out about it and they'll make some sort of a jump there. I've got an old pair of ski-jump skis that the kids just say, 'How can you pick those up?' because they're heavy. And they're long."[38]

The Origins of Hogadon Ski Area

Bob Hardesty shared how skiers began gravitating to the Hogadon hills.

I can't remember all the people that were there, that you had to ski from the old Nursery, the old road. We skied over and then we skied down Park Avenue. Then we skied up the run-out to Boomerang on up through the trees there. Then we skied, sidestepped, whatever you want to call it, then back up Boomerang.

I can remember I had a golden retriever, and I took her along. Hah! When we were going up Boomerang, the snow was deep and her chest was— it was a warm day, but her chest was all covered with snow. So, I took my T-shirt off and I put that on her and tied it up for her. Then, of course, we had to ski back to our cars there. That's when we decided to put Hogadon in.[39]

Although there was quite a lot of mountain real estate devoted to skiing by the mid-1950s, a group composed of leaders of the ski community, Casper businessmen, and the chamber of commerce decided to explore whether there was a new spot that might accommodate a full range of runs, from beginner to expert. This community group established itself as the Central Wyoming Ski Corporation on June 6, 1958, and went to work on creating the Hogadon Ski Area.

Some of the ski organizers included Rob Robertson, Stu Gildersleeve, Tom Stroock, and John Wold, who were all part of both the ski and business communities. Ed Boland represented the businessmen. The group elected John Wold as president, Don Burgess as vice president, John Gee as secretary, and Frank Morgan as treasurer.

The incorporation notice, posted in the Casper papers on June 19, 1958, listed all stakeholders and described what the Central Wyoming Ski Corporation would do to make the Hogadon dream a reality. It promised to build ski runs and buildings, install a tow, and purchase all necessary equipment.[40] The images to the right describe the corporation and its goals and list all of the original members.

NOTICE OF INCORPORATION

NOTICE IS HEREBY GIVEN that the CENTRAL WYOMING SKI CORPORATION has been incorporated in the State of Wyoming by filing its Articles of Incorporation in the Office of the Secretary of State of the State of Wyoming, on the 19th day of June, 1958. The purpose for which said corporation is formed is to encourage, develop and promote interest and participation in skiing and all winter sports by the public generally; to establish, maintain and operate an area and facilities for skiing and winter sports of all kinds in Central Wyoming, to include, but not by way of limitation, roads, trails, hills, mountains, courses, j u m p s, machinery, equipment, ski lifts and tows of all kinds, houses, shelters, buildings, electric and telephone lines, and sanitation facilities; to buy, lease, sell, use and in any other way acquire or dispose of property, both real and personal, in order to carry on any of the aforesaid purpose; to take generally any action whatever to promote, facilitate, or accomplish any of the purposes described above.

This is the incorporation notice for the Central Wyoming Ski Corporation. It shows all of the original members of the group that formed Hogadon. *(Weaver-Hunt collection)*

The amount of capital stock of this corporation shall be $100,000, consisting of 100,000 shares of common stock having no par value, and its term of existence shall be 50 years. The names of the directors who shall manage the concerns of this corporation for the first year, or until the next annual election are Richard L. Armstrong, Edward M. Boland, Howard Bronsdon, Don Burgess, Richard W. Crick, Chaillos Cross Jr., William F. Drew, Robert E. Dove, Glen L. Faulkner, Thomas R. Felt, J. W. Gee, Stewart Goldersleeve, L. M. Grace Jr., George L. Gray, G. W. Hales Jr., W. W. Haines Jr., Robert Hardesty, Henry A. Hitch, D. W. Johnson, David Kidd, Wm. G. Ladd, G. William Mallick, J. D. Milliken, Frank A. Morgan Jr., Angus M. Morrison Jr., Warren A. Morton, Robert E. Nussbaum, George W. Peak, Don Perry, Brendan Phibbs, Richard Poitras, R. M. Robertson, Davis A. Scott, Anne Selden, Thomas F. Stroock, John R. Vorhies, T. H. Walker, Warren B. Weaver, W. E. West Jr., Todd White, John S. Wold, Travis T. Womack Jr. The operations of the corporation will be conducted in each county of the State of Wyoming, and outside of said state, with its principal place of business in this state being Casper, Natrona County, Wyoming, and the name of the agent in charge thereof is J. W. Gee.

CENTRAL WYOMING SKI CORPORATION.

By John S. Wold, President.

P'   : June 25, 26, 27, 1958.

Left: **Tom Stroock was a Casper oilman, politician, and one of the founders of Hogadon Ski Area.** *(Western Heritage Center collection)* Right: **John Wold was another Casper businessman who led in the establishment of Hogadon Ski Area. He was also active in both Wyoming and national politics, becoming the first geologist in the US Congress.** *(Source: Wikimedia)*

In his oral history interview, Tom Stroock recalled how the group decided who was going to divide up tasks and responsibilities.

So anyhow, at that meeting, you pledged money. Then John went over this thing and assigned details to everybody. I remember he assigned the finance route, he and Henry Hitch, who was one of the big stud ducks there. Stu and I were land men, Stu for Atlantic Refining Company and me for the old Standard Oil &Gas. He assigned us for checking out the titles and trying to buy the land. John Voorhees and Trey Womack were in a map company, so they made the maps. Bob Nesbaum, who knew everybody in the ski area— Bob was chasing all over as a skier. He was quite a social bug. They assigned him the job of finding some skier who'd come over and help us locate the area. I do not know how Nes got to meet Peter— what's his name? The guy who discovered the ski area. From Vail.[41]

John Wold and Bob Nesbaum hired Pete Seibert to come up and help them. Seibert, who had been in the 10th Mountain Division in World War II, was working as the ski area manager at Aspen Highland and planning a new ski development at Vail.[42] Seibert was one of the most important figures in the history of the recreational ski industry in the American West.

Lee Grace had been a fighter pilot in World War II and owned a small plane. He took Seibert up to look for possible ski area sites. Grace took him out on a flying survey of land near Casper to see if there was one section that might make a good ski area. They flew over the Ferris Mountains, the Green Mountains, and over parts of the Laramie Range. On the way back to Casper, Seibert looked down at the north side of Casper Mountain and saw a likely spot, where Hogadon now stands, and said, "Here it is right in your own backyard."[43] Seibert was concerned because the ski area would be upside-down. You skied from the top instead of taking the lift up to where you started to ski. That had only worked in a handful of other ski areas.

Peter Seibert's opinion was important, but he was not necessarily the first to notice the Hogadon area's potential. Lee Grace recalled skiing with Barry Horn, who first took him on a cross-country trip to what would later become Hogadon. There was an informal trail down the hill so they skied it. He also remembered Rob Robertson, Stu Gildersleeve, Don Burgess, Howard Bronsdon, and Buck Weaver all skiing with them there on subsequent occasions.[44] Bob Kidd remembered driving in a Jeep over to the top of Hogadon sometime around 1956 or 1957. His dad pointed out the area as the perfect location for a new ski area.[45]

Even though Hogadon represented the transition of skiing on Casper Mountain to a commercial operation, its initial financing was very much a community enterprise. Tom Stroock remembered that the corporation held a social downtown one evening and had people at a table selling shares.

So, you went up that night at the table, Merv and Phyllis Hardesty being there. I remember Marta Stroock being there. The gals signed you up and you pledged to buy so many shares. Twenty-five or two hundred or whatever it was. I remember the big spenders were John [Wold] himself and Ed Boland. I think Ed bought a couple of thousand shares. Marta and I, it was all we could do, we bought a hundred shares and pledged to another hundred. We finally got up I think to three hundred shares. But for us that was a big deal. And for most of the young couples there, it was too.[46] The investors bought anything from a few to hundreds of shares, trying to reach the total amount of $100,000.[47] The stock offer circular went out to potential investors on June 1, 1959.[48]

At the time the shares went public, they had still 99,500 shares for sale. Each share cost one dollar. By November 1959, a report from the corporation showed the following.

To date there are 47,000 shares of stock outstanding, of which 38,000 shares have been sold for cash to approximately 250 individuals; 1,500 shares have been issued for the purchase of land, and 7,500 shares have been issued as payment for work on the area by contractors. The Finance Committee believes that it will be necessary to sell for cash 15,000 more shares of stock in order to begin operations. After this amount is sold, no more of the present issue will be available.[49]

Selling the stock certificates went slowly at first, despite the fact that each share only cost one dollar. To ensure that there was enough money to get the area up and running, the end date for initial stock sales was December 3, 1959. There was an outside investment group waiting in the wings to purchase the remaining stock. This group would have the majority control of management of the ski area. The original founders were hoping to keep most of the control with the core group of skiers.

The Central Wyoming Ski Corporation linked the new ski area to Casper Mountain's history, both financially and symbolically. The company named the new project Hogadon after John Hogadone, who had pioneered the road that ran up the canyon that was becoming the ski area. There may have been two reasons that they gave it that name. One was that Hogadone originally owned some of the land. The other was that Hogadone's daughter had married a man who later went on to be a ski instructor in Sun Valley.[50]

Part of the land they bought was also part of Nils Fougstedt's Dreadnaught claim. As they considered names for the new ski runs, they decided to keep the Dreadnaught name since it had historical links to both Fougstedt and Hogadone and because they thought it might inspire skiers.

The Finance Committee report gave details of what had already been accomplished between June and November. According to John Wold, they wanted to raise $80,000 for all land, buildings, and equipment. The T-bar lift cost $70,000 of that money after they talked the builder, Ernest Constam, down from the $80,000 he originally wanted.[51] He handled the smaller payment by building a shorter tow that did not come as far up the slope as the corporation originally wanted.

The only roadblock to opening on December 15, 1959, was the lack of snow. But everyone was hopeful.[52] While the December 3, 1959, Casper Mountain Ski Association minutes did not mention the state of the snow, it did document most of the other preparations. A report from the corporate officers did provide an update.

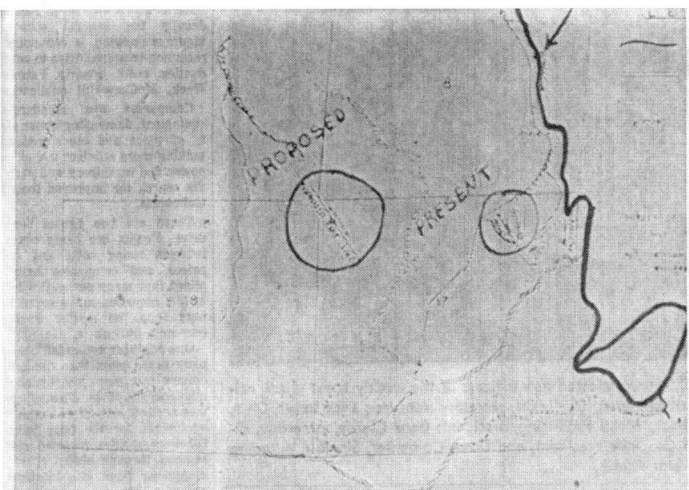

PLANS FOR SKI IMPROVEMENTS IN CASPER AREA GOING FORWARD: The newly-formed Central Wyoming Ski Corporation has set a goal of $60,000 to build facilities at a new ski site (large circle), located three-quarters of a mile west of the present area (small circle). The venture is to begin this fall, and is expected to become Wyoming's second finest ski area—(Tribune-Herald Photo).

Goal of $60,000 Scheduled For Local Ski Improvements

"If the $60,000 goal can be reached, Casper will become one of the most important winter sports areas in this region, stated Casper geologist John S. Wold yesterday in announcing plans of the newly formed Central Wyoming Ski Corporation to build additional ski facilities and runs on Casper Mountain.

The corporation's building program, slated to begin this fall, will make Casper Mountain the second largest ski area in Wyoming, Wold said. But, he added, the venture can be successful only if the support of everyone interested in such recreational facilities is gained. The corporation will market shares of stock at $1 per share to raise the necessary funds.

Thad Walker, corporation board member, said yesterday a few monied skiers will not be carrying the entire load, and he hopes the whole community will come through with its full-fledged support. "It is necessary that everyone interested in the venture contribute as much as possible," Walker stated, "because without the support of the town and small investors, we're dead!"

A public meeting will be held in the council chambers of the City-County building Wednesday at 8 p.m. to outline the plans and needs of the corporation. According to Wold, who is president of the corporation, Casper skiers have realized the inadequacy of the present ski facilities on Casper Mountain, and as a result, there has been some exploratory work going on for almost eight years to develop new slopes there.

Fifteen months ago, a group of interested skiers in Casper donated enough money to bring a professional ski development man, Pete Siebert of Aspen, Colo., to Casper to study possible ski improvements on Casper Mountain. A nationally recognized ski expert, Siebert was chosen by the local group as the best qualified to make an appraisal of the ski possibilities in this area.

Siebert spent several days in the local region looking over ski possibilities, and he picked a site on Casper Mountain about three-quarters of a mile west of the present ski slopes as the best ski area within a 50-mile radius of Casper.

The hill selected by Siebert has a 560-foot vertical drop and offers runs up to one-half mile in length. The terrain will afford slopes for beginners, intermediate and expert skiers and it promises easier access than the present rope tows being used.

Temporary officers of the corporation are Wold, president; Don Burgess, vice president; John Gee, secretary, and Frank Morgan, treasurer. A non-profit organization, the corporation offers no stock options to those working on the project, and no renumeration for the time and effort put into work.

Casper Tribune-Herald, 1959

Status of Central Wyoming Ski Corporation Facility
November 20, 1959

1. Excellent county road to area complete.
2. Three ski trails 95% cleared and graded.
3. T-bar lift 90% completed.
4. Electrical power lines completed to lift area.
5. Temporary warming hut to be completed by December 1.
6. Rest Room facilities and ski patrol shack 75% completed.
7. Parking area graded.
8. Beginners' slopes 100% cleared and graded.
9. Beginners' rope tow 60% completed.
10. Area will be ready to use after December 15 if we have enough snow and if we have enough money to begin operation of the lift.[53]

Left: **Early view of the T-bar at Hogadon** *(Glenn Bochmann collection)* Bottom: **First view of Hogadon, 1959** *(Glenn Bochmann collection)*

Al Haines, Bill Mallick, Don Burgess, Don Perry, Scotty Gray, Dick Schirk, and Dr. Brendan Phibbs trying out Hogadon, 1959 *(Glenn Bochmann collection)*

On February 1, 1960, John Wold sent out a letter to all stockholders announcing the dedication ceremonies for Hogadon would be held on Sunday, February 14. Not only were they inviting stockholders but also the governor, all Wyoming congressional representatives, and city and county officials. He acknowledged that the governor and federal officials would probably not be able to attend. The twenty-minute program honored all those who helped create the ski area.[54]

NOTES

1. Marge Stuckenhoff, Casper Mountain Ski History Project, interview by Sam Weaver, September 26, 2010, 1.
2. Stuckenhoff, interview, 6.
3. Warren Weaver, Casper Mountain Ski History Project, oral history interview by Sam Weaver, November 15, 2009, 3.
4. Angus Morrison, Casper Mountain Ski History Project, oral history interview by Sam Weaver, April 7, 2009, 1–2.
5. Neal Forsling, memoirs.
6. Ole Fougstedt, diary, 1942.
7. Ole Fougstedt, diary, 1942.
8. Ole Fougstedt, diary, entries for January 1943.
9. Ole Fougstedt, diaries, February and March 1943.

10. Ole Fougstedt, diary, March 1943.

11. Bob Kidd, e-mail interview on the early ski school, August 24, 2019.

12. Tom Stroock, Casper Mountain Ski History Project, oral history interview by Sam Weaver and Sean Ellis, n.d., 3.

13. John Hendrickson, "Sideliners," Tribune-Herald Sports, *Casper Tribune-Herald*, September 5, 1946, 6.

14. Hendrickson, "Sideliners," 6.

15. Glenn Bochmann, Casper Mountain Ski History Project, oral history interview by Sam Weaver, April 25, 2011, 7–8.

16. Bill Ladd, Casper Mountain Ski History Project, oral history interview by Sam Weaver, November 22, 2014, 3.

17. Frank (Pinky) Ellis, Casper Mountain Ski History Project, oral history interview by Sam Weaver, January 3, 2014, 4.

18. Morrison, interview, 8.

19. Hendrickson, "Sideliners," 6.

20. Marge Stuckenhoff, interview, 8.

21. Hendrickson, "Sideliners," 6.

22. Ken Hoff and Mike Huber, Casper Mountain Ski History Project, oral history interview by Sandy Leotta and MaryAnn Hoff, March 26, 2019, 2.

23. Mike Huber, Hoff and Huber, interview, 2–3.

24. Charlie Peak, Casper Mountain Ski History Project, oral history interview by Sam Weaver, October 30, 2016, 3.

25. Morrison, interview, 6.

26. *Bulletin*, Casper Mountain Ski Association, December 3, 1959, 1.

27. Bochmann, interview, 4.

28. "Project here recommended by governor," *Casper Tribune-Herald*, n.d., n.p.

29. Peak, interview, 4.

30. Peak, interview, 9.

31. Fred Walters, Casper Mountain Ski History Project, oral history interview by Sam Weaver, October 31, 2015, 2.

32. Peak, interview, 4.

33. Peak, interview, 4.

34. Bochmann, interview, 4.

35. Sam Weaver in Bill and Marilyn Ladd, interview, 12.

36. Ellis, interview, 4.

37. Photograph, *Casper Tribune-Herald*, photograph by Mike Leon.

38. Jim Miller, Casper Mountain Ski History Project, oral history interview by Sandy Leotta and MaryAnn Hoff, 2020, 12.

39. Bob Hardesty, Casper Mountain Ski History Project, oral history interview by Sam Weaver and Sean Ellis, January 3, 2011, 11–12.

40. "Notice of Incorporation," *Casper Tribune Herald*, June 19, 1958.

41. Stroock, interview, 4.

42. Douglas Martin, "Pete Seibert, Soldier Skier Who Built Vail, Is Dead at 77," *New York Times*, July 28, 2002, accessed February 22, 2021, https://www.nytimes.com/2002/07/28/us/pete-seibert-soldier-skier-who-built-vail-is-dead-at-77.html.

43. Lee Grace and Kathy Morton, Casper Mountain Ski History Project, oral history interview by Sam Weaver, 2014, 2.

44. Grace and Morton, interview, 2.

45. Bob Kidd, Casper Mountain Ski History Project, oral history interview by Sam Weaver, November 15, 2014, 4.

46. Stroock, interview, 4.

47. Stock Offer Circular, Central Wyoming Ski Corporation, June 1, 1959.

48. Stock Offer Circular.

49. Tray Womack, Finance Committee Report, November 20, 1959.

50. Morrison, interview, 4–5.

51. John Wold, Casper Mountain Ski History Project, oral history interview by Sam Weaver, July 23, 2010, 3.

52. Finance Committee Report, November 20, 1959.

53. Central Wyoming Ski Corporation status report, November 20, 1959.

54. John Wold, letter to Warren and Sara Weaver from the Central Wyoming Ski Corporation, February 1, 1960.

CHAPTER THREE

Hogadon: Its Space and People

❋ ❋ ❋

Skiers in the early years of Hogadon

*T*HAT'S ONE OF THE THINGS THAT I'VE always found fascinating is the community that developed around making that ski area come to fruition. Everybody volunteered their time and people who had specialties used them to do the work. The people who were landmen were able to acquire the land, do the research, find out who to talk to. The financial people were able to put together the corporation end of it and those things. And the practical people cut trees and did all the things that were necessary to do it. I think that's one of the wonderful things, from my perspective, of looking at this as that community and that volunteerism.

—Lee Grace[1]

The Ski Slopes

The mountain's original runs were cut and prepared by the skiers, starting in 1958. Buck Weaver built a large saw with a circular blade to cut the trees into logs. (Note: The saw was still in use at Weaver's cabin as of 2021.) Dr. Matt Fowler hauled many of the logs out using his four-wheel-drive Jeep. Volunteers cut and split the wood as it came up the hill. They then sold it as firewood, hauling it to town to the buyers. The firewood sales helped pay for Hogadon improvements.

There were other tasks as well. Bob Kidd noted that "I can remember doing my duty as a young rock picker when everybody you've interviewed and others were throwing rocks into the trees. If they were felling trees, you were dragging the limbs. All volunteer work."[2]

As they built the runs, they began to name them. Some names stuck from the beginning, others evolved and changed over time. An early run, called Moneyhill, later became Morning Dew. It was the beginner run. The interview with Bill and Jan Chambers revealed that the ski run names come from historical characters, as well as from contemporary supporters of skiing.

MaryAnn Hoff: "Can you tell me how some of the runs were named?"

This map dating from sometime after 1974 shows the runs at Hogadon. *(Casper Mountain Ski History Project collection)*

Bill Chambers: "I know that Sulley was named after Dr. Sulley, who was unfortunately, he and his daughter were killed in that car wreck. Can't remember the year. [1974] He was a longtime patroller. Patrol leader I think at the time that he was in the fatality on 487. Pattee was named after a miner. Hogadon, as I understand it, was shortened from Hogadone. And the canyon that runs up behind us is Hogadone Canyon. Hogadon, I believe, again was a miner. I'm not sure where Boomerang came from."[3]

In his oral history interview, Angus Morrison recalled that Park and Dreadnaught were some of the later runs built. International Minerals owned the land that was the upper part of Dreadnaught, and the Casper Ski Corporation owned the bottom. Morrison thought they had gotten the city to buy the top piece.[4] According to John Wold, he and Stu Gildersleeve both went to Chicago and talked International Minerals into selling them the land.[5]

Top: **Morning Dew was the second ski run cut by the volunteers.** *(Bob Hardesty collection)* Bottom: **Park Cutoff** *(Bob Hardesty collection)*

Top: **Lower Park Avenue** *(Bob Hardesty collection)* Bottom: **In late 1959, Boomerang was one of the newer runs.** *(Bob Hardesty collection)*

Top: **Dreadnaught, looking up** *(Bob Hardesty collection)* Bottom: **Dreadnaught, looking down** *(Bob Hardesty collection)*   Top: **Lower Holiday** *(Bob Hardesty collection)*

LOWER HOLIDAY

SKI TEAM SLOPE

Bottom: **Upper Holiday** *(Bob Hardesty collection)*   Top: **Ski team slope** *(Bob Hardesty collection)* Bottom: **Pattee** *(Bob Hardesty collection)*

UPPER HOLIDAY

PATTEE

Glenn Bochmann noted that when he and other volunteers were working on cutting Park Avenue, Jack Cowan was the manager. Jack supervised them taking down the trees, and according to the custom of the times, they did not pull out the stumps but cut the trees down to ground level and then left the roots below ground. On the weekends, the ski volunteers came up and they would help cut off the branches and move the trunks to the side. They also laid in logs, parallel to the hill, and then covered them with dirt so the hillside would not get washed out. This worked for many years, until a huge rainstorm washed out all of the logs. They then had to rework the hillside.[6]

There were other issues that challenged slope developers and, eventually, skiers as well. From Charlie Peak in a conversation with Sam Weaver:

Peak: That was the reason that was like that because there's all that water coming out there.

Weaver: Yeah, it was ungodly getting through there with no edges.

Peak: It was quite a challenge. It took the fun out of the run to get down to that bottom.

Weaver: Didn't it have like a creek bed running down there too, if you ran [skied] into the creek down there? If you'd do that at the right time of year, you'd get stuck in the creek sometimes.

Peak: Yeah, they've done a lot of work up there over the years. They had that ice thing in control after a couple years. But I ended up patrolling. I probably started the patrol in '65, '66, in that era. And then I patrolled three or four years. Two years of college, and it wasn't an issue, that glacier down there, so they had taken care of that. But I remember I tried to stay off of Boomerang because every time I'd take a trip down Boomerang, I'd have to bring somebody out with me [laughter]. So, I was avoiding it as much as possible. I remember in those days, there was little pockets of trees scattered all through Boomerang, too. And, of course, no grooming. So, it was all just big moguls and hazards and— Great big moguls. Do you remember

Top: **Park Avenue, showing the log riprap** *(Bob Hardesty collection)* Bottom: **This run was half cleared in the summer of 1959.** *(Bob Hardesty collection)*

Jack Cowan was Hogadon's first manager, between 1959 and 1960.

the tree right in the center of Dreadnaught? And it was a great, big tree. There was actually a little knoll that sticks out now where that tree was, was once. Old George plowed into that tree one time, just hit that sucker head-on. My sister Susan talks about it. I think she was there or was skiing with him. I think the next year they pulled that tree out. It was gone when I was in high school, it was gone.[7]

Once the ski runs were done, there needed to be people to run things. At first, the Casper Mountain Ski Corporation board assigned everyone areas of responsibility, which worked well in the early days. Each member agreed to be the president for a year. That spread out responsibility and let the public know who to contact with questions, praise, or blame.[8] Eventually, there needed to be one person to manage both operations and the physical space. So, the board set out to hire a manager.

Management and Manager

Finding managers took up a lot of time. The first man they hired was Jack Cowan, who ran operations for the 1959–60 season. Cowan came from Dubois, but he had grown up in Casper. He was the son of Frank and Grace Cowan. When Jack became the manager, he started a formal ski school. He borrowed ski instruction books that Angie Morrison had brought back from Alta, Utah, to help him set up the school.[9]

Initially, Cowan also ran the ski corporation's Ski Swap Shop out of his garage. It held adult and kid ski clothes and equipment. By 1960, Jack split his time between his Hogadon job, running the ski school, and running a ski shop, called The Skier, which he had opened on Center Street in Casper. He also had his volunteer duties with the National Ski Patrol, Northern Division. At the end of the 1960–1961 season, he decided to give up being the ski area manager and ski school director to focus on the other parts of his life.[10]

When Jack Cowan left, the corporation brought in Bill DePaemelere, from Colorado, as a temporary manager during the 1961–62 ski season. When he left a year later, DePaemelere went back to Colorado and helped lay out runs at Winter Park and Powderhorn.[11]

Bob Hardesty began to work as the Hogadon manager in the fall of 1962 and continued for the next ten years.[12] Bob was born in 1928 in Cody, Wyoming. His dad was a Methodist minister, so they moved around quite a bit. He had two sisters, Clara Jean and Wilma, who both also skied. His older brother, Charles, was in the 10th Mountain Division. When they moved to Casper in 1940, he skied on the hills at Washington Park and his family skied at Nursery from 1940 until the war. During the war, the road was rarely plowed in winter, so Bob and his friends got one of their dads to drive them up as far as he could get, and then they walked the rest of the way. Sometimes, they only got as far as the Dugway; sometimes, they got all the way to Nursery. They then skied at Nursery and all over the top of the mountain. To get home, they skied to town, using the unplowed road.[13]

Bob married Phyllis, who was also a longtime skier. She raced and taught in the Hogadon ski school for many years.

After Hardesty left, Bob Spickard ran Hogadon for the 1972–73 season. He shared the duties of being in charge of lifts with Gary Vantrease.[14] He also was a ski instructor.

Fred Klein replaced Spickard and was manager until 1978. Klein originally came from the Sinks Canyon Ski Area near Lander to work at Hogadon in 1968. He had first served on the ski corporation board. He moved to the mountain in

Top: **Bob Hardesty was the Hogadon manager from 1962 to 1972.** (*Bob Hardesty collection*) Right: **Phyllis Hardesty** (*Glenn Bochmann collection*) Left: **Bob Spickard, manager, 1972–73** (*Photograph by Glenn Bochmann*)

1972, settling in a geodesic dome built just off of the Hogadon Road.[15] Bob Jones, who had worked at Red Lodge, Montana, worked for Klein as the mechanic and slope packer. In 1975, Jones married Patty Weaver and moved back to Red Lodge.[16]

Dave Furlong followed as manager from 1978 to 1990, assisted by Bob Leroy.[17] He was originally hired by Ed Boland to assist Fred Klein. Boland had bought out the other shareholders and was trying to run the ski area at a profit. When Boland realized he could not reap the profits he wanted, he sold to the city. Furlong stayed on as manager after the city took over.[18] Furlong lived in the manager's apartment in the A-frame attached to the end of the ski lodge.[19]

Gary Vantrease worked at Hogadon for twenty-two years, from 1990 to 2012. He started there after being laid off from the uranium industry. He was lift operation supervisor and then administration supervisor until he became the area manager. He was there when snowboarding first came to Hogadon.[20] Kurt Wenger was the outside operations manager during some of this time.[21]

In 2013, after Gary Vantrease retired, Chris Smith became the new manager. He not only managed the ski area but kept his hand in with the ski school and the Casper Mountain Racers. Over time, Smith went on to help build a new and even better Hogadon Basin Ski area. He is still the manager in 2021.

Chris Smith, Hogadon manager, 2013– (Casper Star-Tribune; photograph by Tom Dixon)

The Buildings

Bob Hardesty remembered that there was a small A-frame building there to warm up skiers and possibly store some equipment. He said,

> See, they moved that over when they started Hogadon. They moved it over there and put it over the toilets down at the bottom, right at the top of Dreadnaught. That became— they moved it up the hill and the ski patrol used it for a while. Then when they moved it up, it set behind the back of the building. If I remember correctly, I think Glen Bochmann [Jack Cowan] had a ski shop there. Then they moved it around in front. It seemed to me that's where the ski school [was]. Finally, they moved it over behind the T-bar, and it sat there and they used it for the ski patrol.[22]

Again, from Angus Morrison:

> The first warming hut there was a big tin building with a big potbellied stove in it. It was down about where the top of Dreadnaught is on the left-hand side. Then down off to the right, where you go down around that tree to get into that gully, they had an A-frame down there that they brought over from Bumps-a-Daisy hill and used that for the ski patrol. They had the toilets in the bottom part of it. Well, Ed's [Boland] wife— we'd always been trying to get him to change the location of where the restrooms was. And they had the lodge already built there then that's there now, with no toilets in it.
>
> So, we tried to get him to go up. But he said, "No." He said, "We don't need somebody running down there to use the toilets. We need the skiers up here." So anyway, his wife had to take her two little kids down there in snow about that deep. She got up there, and next day the work got started on bringing the toilets up the hill [laughs].

The lodge was designed by Hal Engstrom. There was a central fireplace to warm up the skiers. *(Glenn Bochmann collection)*

Did they build the lodge and that stuff down closer to the top of Dreadnaught because of the land deal with International Minerals? It could have been, but the biggest part was the plan they had was they were going to do this lodge here and then move everything up to where the ticket office is and everything all in one building. Well, never had enough money to do anything, so that's the way it is now.[23]

When Engstrom built that, he said that that lodge, he was going to design it so they could add another second floor to it. I don't know wherever they got the idea, but somebody said they couldn't build on top of it, but that whole building is reinforced with steel.[24]

Kathy Morton remembered that the first bathrooms were outhouses that someone had named Jane and John.[25]

John Wold noted that when they held a dedication ceremony for the head house for the T-bar, "They announced: 'Honoring Jane Wold and John Wold, we have named the two johns, the male John and the female Jane, one is named John and other one Jane. You can take a look at the names over the door going in. And I know you'll find it very comfortable in there.' [laughter] That was a substitute for getting a particular trail named after you."[26]

Among the amenities in the lodge was a snack bar. Seating was on picnic tables that the Hogadon managers borrowed from the county parks for the winter.[27] In the 1960s, Jewell Cummings of the Wa-Wa Lodge ran the grill. She also continued to offer food at Wa-Wa. Her offerings were simple, mainly hamburgers, hot dogs, and chili. Later, in the 1970s, Jewell's daughter-in-law, Muriel Street, also ran the grill. She called it The Hogadon Lunch Hutch.[28] By that time, there had been renovations to the lodge, so the space was much nicer.

GOOD EATING
At Hogadon Basin

JEWELL CUMMINGS
is running the
concession!

and the
WA-WA
Pancake House
will open early
in the Spring.

Top left: Jewell Cummings's ad for the Hogadon snack bar *(Julie York collection)* Top right: These picnic tables were borrowed from the county parks department for the ski season. *(Bob Hardesty collection)* Left: Muriel Street in the new kitchen at Hogadon *(Julie York collection)*

Left: **The manager's apartment at Hogadon was part of a set of additions to the lodge.** *(Glenn Bochmann collection)* Bottom left: **Early ski patrol building at Hogadon** *(Gay Nations collection)* Bottom right: **Early ski school building** *(Glenn Bochmann collection)*

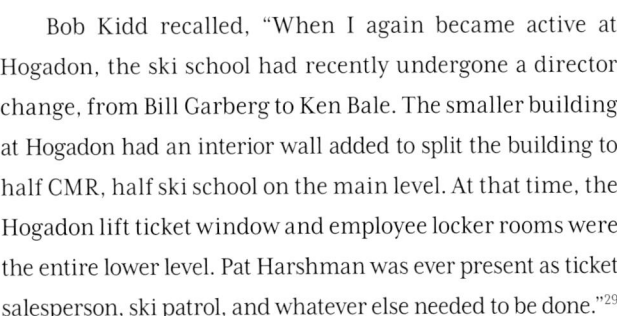

Bob Kidd recalled, "When I again became active at Hogadon, the ski school had recently undergone a director change, from Bill Garberg to Ken Bale. The smaller building at Hogadon had an interior wall added to split the building to half CMR, half ski school on the main level. At that time, the Hogadon lift ticket window and employee locker rooms were the entire lower level. Pat Harshman was ever present as ticket salesperson, ski patrol, and whatever else needed to be done."[29]

The Second Ski Patrol building

MaryAnn Hoff and Bill and Jan Chambers shared what they knew about building the new patrol hut.

MaryAnn: We talked a little bit about the A-frame and the ski patrol hut. It was very basic. When that went away and we got the next patrol hut, who built that?

Bill: I don't know. The Hogadon people may have. I know that we were in there painting and Gay Nations made a lot of stuff. Mike Keim was up there with his power paint machine.

MaryAnn: Well, Hogadon built it, kind of, but then the patrol had to go in and carpet and cupboards and curtains.

Jan: I think Gay Nations built the benches and the radio.

Bill: He and Bob Wheeler, Charlie Koritnik [and Bill Chambers] just worked and worked and worked on that.[30]

Chris Smith, the current manager at Hogadon, noted how the modern ski patrol building functioned.

> The basement of the patrol hut is three sections. We have a section

Top: **Working inside the second ski patrol building** *(Gay Nations collection)* Bottom: **Doubling the size of the ski patrol building. This addition added a kitchen and bathrooms.** *(Gay Nations collection)* Right: **Casper Mountain Ski Patrol members Ralph Barton, Gay Nations, Sean Ellis, Jerry Schilling, Robert Walker, and Bill Bays outside of the second patrol building. This building was in use until 2017.** *(Photograph by Gay Nations)*

where we keep our fencing and things like that in the summertime and a few other odds and ends. Then Spectra, the people that run the concession, they seem to be growing larger into the basement. Then [ski] patrol has a small area in the basement that is mostly the ski area's equipment. They keep calling it theirs, but they could do better if they just moved it over to my side and did something that they want to do down there. But the three of us occupy that.[31]

Equipment

The corporation put in the T-bar just before opening Hogadon in the 1959–60 season. The T-bar cost $70,000 because it was not new. Glenn Bochmann remembered that when he was the T-bar operator, he had to constantly yell at riders to quit swinging the bar. He also noted that the seats often had oil on them from the pulley, and riders complained that their ski pants got oil on them.[32] There was also one seat that did not lower properly when there was a light rider on it. Glenn's son Eric loved to ride that one and then spin around on it.[33]

Bruce Ladd shared a story about doing repairs on the T-bar. Whenever the T-bar broke down, Hardesty would put on his light-blue coveralls and start trying to figure out what

had gone wrong that time. After an hour or so, if he had not fixed it, he would say, "I gotta call Buck [Weaver]," who would come over and help. Then two things happened. The ski day was over, and Buck fixed the problem.[34]

The Poma Lift

Originally, there was a rope tow on Morning Dew, the bunny slope. In the mid-1960s, Hogadon's management decided to replace the rope tow. So, Bob Hardesty drove to Colorado and picked up the tow. "Whether it was Breckenridge—I think it was Breckenridge—or else Steamboat, where we went down."[35] Lee Grace clarified where and how the Hogadon management got the Poma lift for Morning Dew: "I can recall one bit. Bob Hardesty, Don Burgess, and I; I flew them to Steamboat, where, through the grapevine, we heard that there had been a Poma lift available from the Steamboat ski area. We flew down there, looked [at] it, bought it, and shipped it up here. We installed it, and that would be [on] what's now Bumps-a-Daisy? Nursery?

Top: **This is the top of the T-bar in 1960. It did not quite come all the way up the hill. Ernie Constam had built it too short because the ski corporation could not afford the full $80,000 asking price.** (Glenn Bochmann collection) Bottom: **This is the bottom of the T-bar.** (Bob Hardesty collection)

Bunny slope. That was about three or four years after we started the main ski area. It all goes back to volunteer work. That was the attraction of it."[36]

Chairlifts

Hogadon got chairlifts after the city bought the area. There were two originally, one on Dreadnaught and one on Boomerang. Later, they tore out the Boomerang chair.[37]

Cam Walker also remembered that Brandeth Hand was a skier who was injured when the chair she and Angus Morrison were riding on fell off the lift. She fell on Angie's legs and broke both of his legs. She came out of the accident with minor injuries. The chair came off because someone forgot to replace a cotter pin.

Packing the Slopes

As we have seen, in the earliest years, on the older slopes, groups of skiers were the original slope packers. At many ski areas, including at Hogadon, a ski manager both could and did offer young skiers a chance to get a free pass for arriving early and spending part of the morning ski packing the slopes. Bob Hardesty remembered the season he spent in Sun Valley, where he paid for a whole season of skiing by packing in the morning and skiing in the afternoon. As he said, "After I found my way around, if you were at the bottom of River at 8:30 in the morning, you could ride up, get to the top of the mountain. They'd have a ski patrolman with you. There might be fifteen, twenty, maybe twenty-five people. They'd take you out on the hill, line you up, and then you'd just sidestep down the hill to pack." Bob recreated that when he managed Hogadon.[38] He described how he got high school kids to pack for him. "But there were high school kids, if they met me at the old armory about eight o'clock in the morning, I'd take them up the mountain with me. I'd get some of them to go over, shovel moguls, but also on the T-bar,

Riders on the chairlift *(Glenn Bochmann collection)*

because it would drift in, you had to cut the drift out to get the T-bar up. They'd shovel that."[39]

Bob Hardesty remembered the first mechanical packer they used at Hogadon.

> The Bradley Packer came from Winter Park. Bob and Fred Klein picked it up and brought it to Hogadon. Fred was the only one who used it. It had a wheel with spokes on it, wooden wheel. Had boards across there, then it had a plow in front and rigged up where you'd ride in front of it for cutting moguls. We never used it that much. And Fred was the only one that had enough guts— you're clear up in front and then there were pieces of metal out in front. Then between where you stood and back, there's a little plow. You could crank and it would drop a blade to cut the top of the moguls. Then you'd go straight down the hill, and you'd raise or lower that blade. I never did run it. And we didn't use it that much.[40]

Bill Ladd gave another description of both Fred and the Bradley Packer that they called Sweet Pea.

> He went down [to] Winter Park and got hold of— there was guy down there that had invented this packer that you hauled behind. I can't remember his name. Steve something. He was able to buy one, Fred Klein was, and brought it up there. He would run up and down the hill, packing the slope with that packer. I don't know what ever happened to that.[41]

Ladd did not clarify how they got it back up the hill. Perhaps they attached it to the T-bar and dragged it up.

There were other kinds of equipment that they acquired to groom the slopes. Generally, the corporation bought used gear. In the early days, the machinery was pretty simple, but as the number of slopes grew, so too did the need for more versatile equipment. Bob Hardesty documented some of what they used over the years. One piece of equipment was a Dodge Power Wagon that they used to plow the parking lot, usually at night. He could also tow circular cages that helped smooth out the runs.

> Then we got the old Christy Cat. We cut it apart and I'd pull it up and down the hill in this old Christy

Fred Klein grooms the slope using a human-powered Bradley Packer, affectionately called Sweet Pea. (*Photograph by Glenn Bochmann*)

This is the newest maintenance building. It was one of the new structures that came online in 2017. (*Hogadon Basin Ski Area collection*)

Cat. It was quite a machine. It was a fiberglass body, and it had a Volkswagen engine in it. But what you could do in that— and it had a hydraulic, so if you were going across the hill, you could go on across the hill, you could move it one way or the other and it set like this.

> Then if you turned around, you could turn it. Used to run that up and down Dreadnaught and Park Avenue. Then, I'd pack up there with that. That's what I used for packing.[42]

Becoming a City Ski Area

In the fifteen years that Hogadon was a corporate operation, the company made a small profit almost every year. However,

THIOKOL SPRYTE

TUCKER SNOCAT

Top left: **The Thiokol Sprite** *(Glenn Bochmann collection)* Top right: **The Tucker Snocat** *(Glenn Bochmann collection)* Left: This building at Hogadon came from the Asbell construction company, which built the first lodge. They got it at the airport at Barr Nunn. It later became the maintenance building. *(Glenn Bochmann collection)* Bottom: Grooming equipment *(Glenn Bochmann collection)*

by the late 1960s, the original investors wanted out of running the ski area. After Ed Boland bought everyone else out, he promised his investors a tidy return on their investments, but costs were high and the profits were low. And to make matters worse, the old, used T-bar was becoming dangerous.

Bill Garberg noted in his interview that he and his father-in-law, Hub Hubble, met with Casper's city manager, Ken Erickson, to propose that the city buy Hogadon. Erickson was interested but needed to do a bit of research. To aid in that, Bill and Hub went to Colorado and met with some of the directors of Winter Park Ski Area. Since it was owned and run by the City and County of Denver, they had some perspective. The Winter Park managers gave them documentation on their area and how they ran it. City Manager Erickson used that documentation to prepare a presentation to the city council. As part of the process, he created a commission that included Don Burgess, John Wold, Lee Grace, and Rob Robertson. One of their proposals was for the ski area to buy a new lift, this time a chairlift. The deal ultimately involved a transfer of property in exchange for the ski area.

Pinky Ellis gave a description of the deal from his perspective.

> The big difference was in the city acquiring the property. I felt I had at least a vote on that. On the city council at that time, Art Volk and Bob Johnson, who owned the Kassis store, and myself were all members and strong advocates of skiing. By that time, Hogadon really was in disarray and trying to keep it financed. That's an entirely different story.
>
> So anyway, we were the ones that voted to make the exchange with the corporation of the property they owned up there, and what we offered and they accepted at the time were two lots in what is now part of Robert Taylor's stuff. But the city had acquired it.
>
> As it turned out, the two lots were sold, and it was the way a lot of the original investors recovered their monies. Jackie and I had made a modest little

contribution. I don't remember it was anything very big, $500 or something like that on the prospects that our kids would be able to learn to ski there, and we got our money back. We didn't lose anything. That was fascinating.

> But I do think that that was worthwhile. We convinced the city manager that this would be a pretty good deal, and he was able to have some enthusiasm in presenting it to the rest of the council. And I think it was worth it. I'm glad to see now that currently, the city has recognized that they really need to do something up there or forget it. They're putting some money into it. This year will be the first year in that new expansion program. I think it's going to be really worthwhile.[43]

Friends of Hogadon

Another piece of the financial puzzle was how to get the community more involved in financing items that Hogadon needed but that were not in the budget. The answer was to create a nonprofit organization called the "Friends of Hogadon." Bob Kidd relates the story of the origins of the organization.

> Your question about the "Friends of Hogadon" has a quick answer, which is: The Summer of 2015, the 501(c)(3) filing was made with the Wyoming secretary of state. The initial funding contribution was made by Bob and Nancy Kidd. Ray Bader, CPA, ski area user, race-athlete parent, volunteer for everything, ski patrol, does CMR and ski patrol books for free; Bruce Lamberson, all things Mountain Sports, Hogadon Rental Shop; Bob Kidd, businessman, former racer, racer parent, racer grandparent, CMR Board of Directors, volunteer CMR coach. The three of us attended countless meetings together that were called OAC Meetings—owners, architects, and contractors for the new Hogadon Lodge. Over time, the three of us became the representatives of the owner/

users of Hogadon. It took a time to get to the point of developing the formal not-for-profit corporation. After being told for months by city council members they needed community buy-in, Bob and Nancy [Kidd] made an effort to write the City of Casper a check earmarked for Hogadon, to discover from City Manager John Patterson and council that no mechanism existed to handle funds.

The "Friends of Hogadon" told the city we would handle furnishings and other amenities so that the Optional 1-Cent Sales Tax money could go entirely to construction of the lodge. We had a good start on fundraising by the time we had the grand-opening fundraiser, August 21, 2017 (the solar eclipse), which raised $13,000. To date, the "Friends" have raised nearly $120,000 for tables and chairs, landscaping, deck furniture, TV monitors with slope-side cameras, boot-up benches, daily and seasonal lockers, ATM machine. The list is long and growing.[44]

Chris Smith added to Bob's story related to the origins of the "Friends" group. According to Smith, it was started by Bob Kidd, Bruce Lamberson, Ray Bader, and David LaPlante. In 2017, it came time to furnish needed items for both the new ski lodge and the ski area, and they raised $85,000. One of their projects, led by Ray Bader, was installing wireless cameras on the runs so that people in the lodge could watch people, including their kids, skiing.[45]

The New Lodge

Chris Smith described where various operations were in the new building in 2019.

It's right next to Snow Sport School, down in the first level, the snow level. It's really nice because the ski school's right here and then the rental shop's right here, so you come down— we sell tickets at the customer service desk just for the ease, just for good customer service. Then people go downstairs, meet their instructors, and then the instructors go through the rental shop with them and walk right out on the snow. It really is a nice facility for that now.[46]

The ski area management and the city contracted out running the restaurant and bar at the lodge to a private company called Spectra. It also ran concessions at the Casper Events Center.[47]

Building the new lodge, 2016–17
(*Photograph by Glenn Bochmann*)

Top: **The new Hogadon lodge** *(Hogadon Basin Ski Area collection)* Left: **This is the dining room in the new lodge.** Right: **The bar area features large windows.**

New Ski Patrol and Snow Sports/CMR Buildings

Top: **The ski patrol building in 2021** (*Geoff Hunt collection*) Bottom: **Snow Sports School and Casper Mountain Racers building, 2021** (*Photograph by Geoff Hunt*)

Plans for the Future

In 2019, Chris Smith noted that he wanted to be manager for another ten years and retire out of the job. His long-term plans included putting in hiking and mountain biking trails for summer use. In 2019, using volunteer labor, they had completed two miles of bike trails. Smith wanted the trails to also be available for high school teams and was planning a five-kilometer loop for racing. Another plan was to put up a wooden gazebo for small weddings and another smaller lodge with a fireplace, kitchenette, and bathrooms, also for weddings and other social gatherings. Both of these were to be rental facilities. Smith also got the ski area designated as a city park so that people could come up and hike in the summer.[48]

As far as equipment goes, Smith is hoping to be able to afford a quad lift to replace the double chair. He also hopes to open up the western ridge beyond Park Avenue to provide a more challenging children's slope. It would have a T-bar tow. He knows that Casper is very community oriented and that, maybe with the help of the "Friends of Hogadon," he can make these dreams come true.[49]

Tune-up Day

One innovation of the past few decades is actually an extension of the old community spirit that was part of each stage of skiing on Casper Mountain. Each year, families come together

Top: **This is from the 2018 Tune-up Day.** (*Hogadon Basin Ski Area collection*) Right: **Trash pick-up** (*Hogadon Basin Ski Area collection*)

Left: Painting the ski shop (*Hogadon Basin Ski Area collection*) Right: Feeding the team (*Hogadon Basin Ski Area collection*) Bottom: The 2014 Tune-up Day volunteers (*Hogadon Basin Ski Area collection*)

in September to clean, paint, mend, and cut firewood to get Hogadon ready for another season. The photographs on pages 73 and 74 show the work going on at the 2018 Tune-up Day.

Skiing at Hogadon – Then and Now

Top: **Dr. Nat Fowler in the City Race.** *(Glenn Bochmann collection)* Bottom: **Don Burgess in the City Race** *(Glenn Bochmann Collection)*

Right: Joyce Garberg, Anker Larsen, Don Chapin, and Marta Stroock in the timing tent *(Glenn Bochmann collection)* Bottom left: Trophy time: Bill Ladd presents a trophy to Ann Stroock. *(Glenn Bochmann collection)* Bottom right: Marie Robertson, gate official, City Race *(Glenn Bochmann collection)*

Opposite page

Top: Hogadon runs in the 1970s *(Phil Cole collection)* Bottom left: Snowboarding on a bluebird day *(Hogadon Basin Ski Area collection)* Bottom right: Hogadon Basin Snow Sports class *(Hogadon Basin Ski Area collection)*

Left: **Relaxing in the Hogadon snack bar** *(Bob Hardesty collection)* Right: **For many years, Della Works brought Easter candy for all of the kids at Hogadon.** *(Della Works collection)* Bottom: **Après ski at the Hogadon Lodge** *(Bob Hardesty collection)*

Hogadon Social Life

Wednesday was the one weekday when people could come up in the afternoon for skiing. It was a way for Casper residents, especially women, to get out during the week. When Kathy Morton went up with Marge Stuckenhoff, Jackie Reasoner, and a few other friends, Kathy's husband, Warren, would occasionally join them. She loved the fact that they mostly had the slopes to themselves and that the lift lines were very short, which they felt made Hogadon so much better than Colorado resorts.[50]

Sometimes, people did things for others, just for fun. The ski patrol auxiliary supplied snacks for patrollers to eat between rescues. Visiting with friends after a long day of skiing cemented friendships that lasted for decades. Also, for many years, Della Works dressed up as the Easter Bunny as she brought candy to all children skiing on Easter.

For decades, the summertime fair and rodeo parade featured a mountain skiing float. In 2008, on the occasion of its fiftieth anniversary, Hogadon also placed a float in the annual Casper Christmas holiday parade.

Top: **Greg Lance, Warren Weaver, and MaryAnn Hoff bring up the rear of the float** *(Hogadon Basin Ski Area collection)* Bottom: **Bob Kidd and Mary Lou Morrison join others on the Hogadon float in the Christmas Parade.** *(Hogadon Basin Ski Area collection)*

Ski Equipment and Ski Fashion

Finding ski gear was always a challenge for Casper skiers, especially in the early years. The generation that started skiing in the 1920s bought wooden skis of Scandinavian design. Many skied with a single pole. Their children made skis from barrel staves fastened onto rubber galoshes using twine. Ted French and other early innovators taught classes in ski making. Eventually, companies like Groswald out of Denver sold skis locally. Kistler Tent and Awning, a Casper store that dated to the beginnings of the town, branched out in the 1930s and opened Kistler Sporting Goods. Ralph Barton recalled that Kistler's was one of the first to carry postwar surplus skis, poles, boots, and clothing.[51] Bill Ladd shared his recollections of the type of surplus gear that Kistler's carried.

Well, it came from the 10th Mountain Division. In fact, there were quite a few guys in Casper that had been in the 10th Mountain Division. But this fellow in north Casper, he had all sorts of army surplus stuff. Ski equipment being part of it.

The skis were real wide because the ski troops were cross-country skiing more than Alpine skiing to get to where they needed to fight. So, they were painted white. The ski clothing was the parkas and the pants, and everything were reversible. They were green on one side and white on the other, so that if they were in snow, they could turn them white side out. The tents, they had mountain tents, had floors in them. Then they had the sleeping bags. The ski poles were probably like cross-country ski poles. They were real tall and the baskets were probably twelve inches wide on the bottom, so they wouldn't sink into the soft snow. The bindings were just cable bindings with a spring on the front, so when you put your boot in the toe piece, you threw the clamp down and it tightened the boot up. We even had army surplus boots.[52]

The Casper Mountain Ski Club ran a ski sale and swap operation, originally out of people's garages, including that of Jack Cowan. The December 3, 1959, CMSA *Bulletin* said, "The ski swap shop is really going to swap this year. Helen Worrall and her bums have it really going. Here is the dope.

 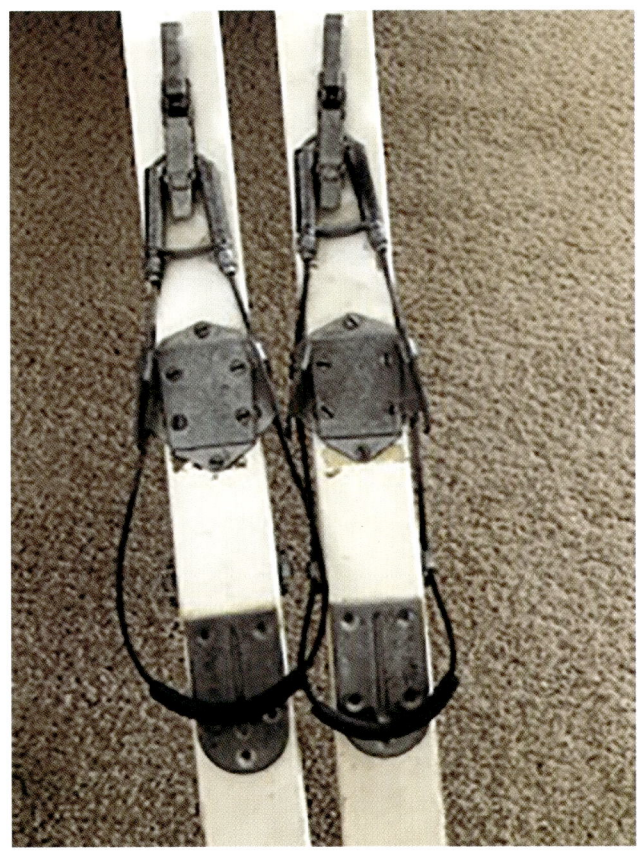

Left: **These are the original bindings used by the first generation of skiers.** *(Ken and MaryAnn Hoff collection)* Right: **10th Mountain Division bindings** *(Ken and MaryAnn Hoff collection)*

Place: Jack Cowan's garage – bring your own. Price: Name your own. Items: All and any – Large or small." It also noted that there would soon be items available at the warming hut at Hogadon. "Items include, wax, bindings, mittens, skis, poles, wine sacks (no wine), clothing, boots."[53] The purpose was twofold: to get people outfitted so they could ski, and to bring in a little money to the ski area to keep things running. Later on, at Hogadon, there was a rental shop at the ski area. In the new Hogadon ski lodge, Mountain Sports manages the rental shop.

From Bill Ladd:

> That got us started, but by the next year, we purchased most of our equipment— there were several places around town, but Kistler Sporting Goods was the— well, they called it Kistler Tent and Awning at the time. They had the canvas shop in the back and in the front—it was on Center Street—they had a sporting goods store. They had ski equipment there.
>
> Well, even the army surplus skis had metal edges. But they were fastened with screws. They weren't embedded into the ski like they are today. So, you were constantly having to repair those edges because they would break off. But even with the skis that we bought from Kistler Tent and Awning, they had a metal edge that screwed on there. Wooden skis. Some of them were made in Denver and some of them they brought in from someplace else. There was a company in Denver called Griswald [Groswald] and they made a ski. That was pretty popular. Then there was a Northland ski, I remember.[54]

Over time, Kistler's would be joined by Jack Cowan's The Skier and then The Ski Shop owned by Glenn and Chris Bochmann. Eventually, Bruce Lamberson's Mountain Sports became the most successful of the ski and sport shops, even taking over running the ski rental shop at Hogadon.

Top: This wool clothing was used by skiers from the 1920s to the 1950s. The ski outfit belonged to Lou Demorest, courtesy of Jan Demorest. The sweaters are from Ken and MaryAnn Hoff. *(Ken and MaryAnn Hoff collection)* Bottom: Square-towed leather ski boots, a wool cap, and aviator sunglasses that were used in the 1950s *(Bob Hardesty collection)*

Barry Horn and Sam Weaver discussed 1950s clothing:

Weaver: What kind of clothing did you have?

Horn: Well. [pause] Kind of ski pants. But they were semi-waterproof [laughs] that way. We used a lot of knee-length and knee stockings, these knit Norwegian stockings that came up. Big rubber bands to hold them up. That was always in style, using the knee socks and the pants. Then sweaters, big knit sweaters, bulky sweaters usually, with a shell over them. I probably skied with a ski patrol jacket almost all the time. They were nothing but a little canvas shell. An orange canvas shell, but it worked. It was good. Hats, knit hats that you pulled down. And goggles.[55]

Charlie Peak noted, "Yeah. Square-toed boots. Beartrap, with the strap over the top. No edges. I mean the edges were something that adults skied with; kids did not have them."[56]

In 1952, Fred Walters and his friends skied in wool ski pants, sweaters, canvas jackets, and various kinds of hats.[57] Ski clothing also reflected fashion trends and new materials. Wool gave way to nylon and leather boots gave way to high-tech plastic. Skis evolved from wood to metal to laminates.

Over the years, the Casper Mountain Ski Club (CMSC) even designed custom club patches and a club sweater with a white *V* on the front. The sweaters stayed the same into the 1960s, but the patch design changed each year. The CMSC *Bulletin* in 1959 reported, "Ski Patches: You know – the pretty ones we all buy and sew on the jacket – well we want a new one— really hot-looking and racy like a missile. Lou Demorest and (Skin Head) Bill Burks, our Captain and Mate, are looking and listening for you guys and dolls to come up with that gray matter, so inform."[58] The patches that had always featured Slalom Sam stayed the same over time, even if his looks changed.

Casper Mountain at Warren Weaver's cabin, 1951–52 ski season. Left to right: Fred Walters, Chuck Morrison, Jerry Cody, unknown, and Bruce Cody. *(Fred Walters collection)*

Top left: Jayne Morton and Virginia Forbes are elegant in the latest fur ski coats. (Casper Star-Tribune, *January 17, 1964*) Top right: Bill Harrison and Art Volk show off the latest ski clothes. (Casper Star-Tribune, *January 17, 1964*) Bottom left: Jackie Reasoner (left) and Pat Lockhart (right) wear the latest in outfits for the 1980s. (*Bruce Ladd collection*) Bottom right: Jerry Surber and Pat Frost sport the official Casper Mountain Ski Club sweater. Howie Bronsdon and Ellen Bundy join for the photograph. (*Bob Hardesty collection*)

Top left: This early Slalom Sam patch dates to the 1930s. *(Bill Bon collection)* Top right: These CMSC patches date from the 1940s. The red patch is an early Slalom Sam. *(Susan Bishop collection)* Left: Chris Bochmann's 1956 ski club column in the *Casper Star-Tribune* used Sam as the mascot. *(Fred Walters collection)* Bottom left: This was the first Slalom Sam patch to say "Hogadon." *(Bob Hardesty collection)* Bottom right: This is the 2021 version of Slalom Sam. *(Hogadon Basin Ski Area collection)*

NOTES

1. Lee Grace and Kathy Morton, Casper Mountain Ski History Project, oral history interview by Sam Weaver, 2014, 3.

2. Bob Kidd, Casper Mountain Ski History Project, oral history interview by Sam Weaver, November 15, 2014, 5.

3. Bill Chambers in Bill and Janet Chambers, Casper Mountain Ski History Project, oral history interview by MaryAnn Hoff and Sandy Leotta, January 31, 2019, 10.

4. Angus Morrison, Casper Mountain Ski History Project, oral history interview by Sam Weaver, April 7, 2009, 11.

5. John Wold, Casper Mountain Ski History Project, oral history interview by Sam Weaver, July 23, 2010, 3.

6. Glenn Bochmann, Casper Mountain Ski History Project, oral history interview by Sam Weaver, April 25, 2011, 6.

7. Charlie Peak interview, Casper Mountain Ski History Project, oral history interview by Sam Weaver, October 30, 2016, 6–7.

8. Lee Grace in Lee Grace and Kathy Morton, Casper Mountain Ski History Project, oral history interview by Sam Weaver, 2014, 5.

9. Morrison, interview, 7.

10. Kidd, interview, 5.

11. Morrison, interview, 12.

12. Hardesty, interview, 14.

13. Hardesty, interview, 1/2.

14. Bill Ladd and Bob Kidd, e-mails, February 10–11, 2021; Morrison, interview, 12.

15. Sandy Leotta, Casper Mountain Ski History Project, oral history interview by MaryAnn Hoff, September 22, 2020, 6.

16. Rebecca Hunt, conversation with Patty Jones, February 28, 2021.

17. Ralph Barton, Casper Mountain Ski History Project, oral history interview by Sam Weaver, March 12, 2012, 11; Chris Smith, Casper Mountain Ski History Project, oral history interview by MaryAnn Hoff and Sandy Leotta, February 7, 2019, 7.

18. Bruce Lamberson, Casper Mountain Ski History Project, oral history interview by MaryAnn Hoff and Sandy Leotta, n.d., 2.

19. Lamberson, interview, 10.

20. Christina Schmidt, "Vantrease: 'Time for me to move on,'" *Casper Journal*, May 2012.

21. Smith, interview 7.

22. Hardesty, interview, 9

23. Morrison, interview, 13.

24. Morrison, interview, 13.

25. Grace and Morton, interview, 3.

26. Wold, interview, 7.

27. Hardesty, interview,16.

28. Julie York, e-mail to Rebecca Hunt, January 23, 2021.

29. Bob Kidd, e-mail to Rebecca Hunt, February 15, 2021.

30. Chambers, interview, 15–16.

31. Smith, interview, 12.

32. Bochmann, interview, 6.

33. Bochmann, interview, 7.

34. Bruce Ladd, Casper Mountain Ski History Project, oral history interview by MaryAnn Hoff and Sandy Leotta, January 23, 2019, 19.

35. Hardesty, interview, 11 and 19.

36. Grace in Grace and Morton, interview, 4.

37. Cam Walker, Casper Mountain Ski History Project, oral history interview by Sandy Leotta and MaryAnn Hoff, March 21, 2019, 4–5.

38. Hardesty, interview, 11.

39. Hardesty, interview, 17.

40. Hardesty, interview, 16.

41. Bill and Marilyn Ladd, Casper Mountain Ski History Project, oral history interview by Sam Weaver, November 22, 2014, 16.

42. Hardesty, interview, 16.

43. Frank (Pinky) Ellis, Casper Mountain Ski History Project, oral history interview by Sam Weaver, January 3, 2014, 11–12.

44. Bob Kidd, e-mail to Rebecca Hunt, February 22, 2021.

45. Smith, interview, 5.

46. Smith, interview, 10.

47. Smith, interview, 16,

48. Smith, interview, 12.

49. Smith, interview, 11.

50. Morton in Grace and Morton, interview, 5.

51. Ralph Barton, Casper Mountain Ski History Project, oral history interview by Sam Weaver, March 31, 2012, 5.

52. Bill and Marilyn Ladd, interview, 11.

53. *Bulletin*, Casper Mountain Ski Association, December 3, 1959, 1.

54. Bill and Marilyn Ladd, interview, 11.

55. Barry Horn, Casper Mountain Ski History Project, oral history interview by Sam Weaver, April 27, 2013, 8.

56. Peak, interview, 6.

57. Fred Walters, Casper Mountain Ski History Project, oral history interview by Sam Weaver, October 31, 2015, 1.

58. *Bulletin*, 1.

CHAPTER FOUR

Ski School, Ski Patrol, and Racing

Jim Colva is in the handles and MaryAnn Hoff is on the tail rope during a rescue practice. *(Photograph by Gay Nations)*

Introduction

*T*ELLING THIS PART OF THE STORY IS COMPLICATED. Love of Alpine skiing led to a desire to be better skiers. A teaching system, at first informal, evolved into formal teaching, first on the slopes scattered over the mountain and then consolidated at Hogadon after 1959. Skiers needed training, not only to make them better at the sport, but also to make them safer on the slopes. To achieve that, the ski community came through again. They sorted themselves into one of two groups, ski instructors or the ski patrol.

As more and more people found the love of skiing (and as Hogadon became more corporate), they hired managers, who then hired the heads of the ski school. Skiers wanted instructors who would take them to higher levels of expertise. And as they became more expert skiers, there was a desire to run races and compete on the local, regional, and national levels. Over time, the ski school divided, and while many continued to teach beginners, some coaches began training different levels of advanced skiers, many of whom were intent on becoming racers. The club's work resulted in the birth of two high school Alpine teams, two Nordic teams, and even a short-lived team at Casper College. And in 1969, the Casper Mountain Ski Club (CMSC) created the Casper Mountain Racers.

At the same time, those drawn to the ski patrol organized—again—a loose structure that coalesced over time into a well-trained group that affiliated with regional and national groups and with local emergency and medical services. As with teaching skiing, teaching rescue and injury care moved from informal to very formal. An all-volunteer patrol force continued but—eventually—with paid leadership. People cared, and working together, they created needed organizational structures built out of the community spirit that had always been part of the ski scene.

Ski Training and the Ski School

In 1935, Cy Bon encouraged the Casper Mountain Ski Club to organize the first ski clinic on the mountain. They brought in Thor Groswald, Tommy Tompkins, and Florian Hamerly,

Ole Fougstedt teaching Debra Street to ski circa 1960 (*Julie York collection*)

a professional ski racer, to train interested skiers in more professional techniques.[1] Thor Groswald owned the Denver-based Groswald Ski Company, which opened in 1932 and virtually controlled the American wooden-ski market for many years. He was a professional racer in both Nordic and Alpine events who brought not only ski techniques but also ski-making technology from his native Norway. Groswald was the co-founder of Arapahoe Basin Ski Area in Colorado and helped form both the Winter Park and Berthoud Pass areas.[2] The ski clinic was a success and fueled an interest in more formal training. It would take about ten years, with a war in the middle of it, to make that a reality. And it was fueled by a younger generation who were ready to fly on the cold, white powder.

Fred Walters moved back to Casper with his mother, Wanda, in 1952. He was ten years old, and that first winter, his uncle Buck Weaver and his mother bought him skis from Kistler Sporting Goods. Buck got a discount since he worked part-time at the store. Fred remembered he had square-toed boots and wooden edges on the skis.[3]

More importantly, Fred remembered that at first, he was like the other young skiers—self-taught. He and his ski buddies, who were Eddie Summerford, Bruce Cody, Rich Armstrong, Billy Kidd, and Bobby Sensentaffer, would get up on the slopes and practice what they saw others doing. But he also noted that there was a dedicated corps of the older generation who

These were the type of skis available in the late 1940s and 1950s. The white ones are World War II 10th Mountain Division surplus. *(Ken Hoff collection)*

took the kids under their wings. These included Don Burgess, Don Perry, Lew Penwell, Rob Robertson, Bob Hardesty, Barry Horn, and, of course, his Uncle Buck.[4] Many of these older skiers went on to found the ski school.

Most of the younger generation mentioned that the first stage was to put on a pair of skis and try them out. Snow plowing was the first, safest technique. It helped you to turn and stop. Then, as they got more confident, they would try a basic parallel move, just to get a bit of speed. This worked well on Nursery, which had a long downhill, then turned flat, and even rose a bit at the end. Watching their friends gave them hints on how to improve further. Barry Horn noted that ski films, magazines, and news reels provided hints.[5] Many of the earliest skiers had been the Boy Scouts who had benefitted from Ted French's training. Some of the newer generation learned from one of French's co-leaders, Bill Haines Sr., and other later scoutmasters.

Angie Morrison shared that when he was at Sun Valley, he got to see and practice the Arlberg method, the *projection circulaire*, modified Austrian techniques, and some newer American techniques that were growing out of the European methods.[6] The Arlberg method utilizes short, sharp turns mostly controlled by the knees and ankles. It is a bit choppy but allows for more controlled speeds. On the other hand, an Arlberg crouch lets a skier speed in a fast—but controlled—fashion. It is especially good for winning downhill races. *Projection circulaire* uses broad sweeping turns, which are graceful and help deal with slope curves and moguls. A modified Austrian technique uses the hips to help stop periodically during straight downhill runs. The hip motion caused the upper edges to dig into the snow, stopping the skier. Modern ski instructors lump all of these styles under the term "ski carving."

Bob Kidd mentioned a ski technique called Tyrolean, which he described as "do a 'kick turn' at the end of a traverse to change directions and traverse in the opposite direction, repeat."[7] Bob later became one of the longest-running instructors, still teaching in 2021.

Angie Morrison and Bill Haines taught kids on Nursery. Each of them would teach about fourteen kids and start them with the snowplow technique, then the basic parallel technique, and then advance them to faster and more intricate moves. When they grew up, some of the Nursery students became early instructors at Hogadon and later coached the Casper Mountain Racers.[8]

In an e-mail interview, Bob Kidd noted that students received patches as they moved up in skill level.

I was young, but I remember the patches only the years the school buses ran and on Nursery. Hogadon was opening in 1958 [1959] and was the focus of attention. If I was ten years old the winter of 1957–58, the school bus shuttle was probably 1954–55–56.

The lessons were very organized along the lines of the 10th Mountain Division (my guess for the names and progression, I felt like I was in the army) and much of the equipment was military surplus. You were very upscale if you had metal edges on your skis and there were many pullover coats that were brown or reversible to snow white for camouflage with a fur hood.

The felt strips in question signified the level of proficiency for skill levels in the ski school. When the child/student could perform the required skill, they would get the ribbon and advance to the next level. Back in the day of our school bus rides to Nursery from the old National Guard Armory, these skill level patches were highly sought after. You would see a bus load of boys and girls with these sewn on the pant leg or coat, it was a real motivator to get to the next level and keep up with the group.

As best I recall:

Yodeler: walk/glide on skis, side step, herringbone up hill, get into a snowplow

Tyrolean: ride the rope tow to the top, traverse the slope, sideslip, get into a snowplow, snowplow stop

Alpiner: snowplow turn, snowplow into a traverse, stem christie, un-weighting into a parallel turn, speed/straight run

Skivalzer: the most important patch to signify you had gained a high level of proficiency in all expected levels[9]

The ski school began as part of the Boy Scouts programs in the early 1950s, when Bill Haines Sr. and Bill Bon ran their Boy Scouts ski school. They taught very basic techniques like the snowplow and the stem christie.[10] But this was only available to boys. When the ski club started to plan for Hogadon, they asked Angus Morrison to go to Alta, Utah, to consult with Alf Engen, who ran the ski school there. A

Ski student badges (*Bob Kidd collection*)

Fred Walters's ski team badge, 1958 *(Fred Walters collection)*

number of the Casper skiers had taken lessons on holidays to Alta and respected Alf's work. Angie came back with training manuals and the certainty that they had to have trained and certified instructors. Angie actually went to Montana to train and get his certification. He was perhaps the first certified ski teacher in Casper. Angie noted that there were three levels of training. When a person got certified, they got a pin for each level.[11]

Angie and Rob Robertson took on the responsibility of organizing that first formal ski school around 1958. They recruited from the ranks of those who had already been teaching, mostly on Nursery. These people included Pat Haines, Dale and Glenn Faulkner, Don Burgess, Bill Peak, and Lou Demorest.[12] They then went on to get certified and to train other instructors.

Early teachers were creative because they had to teach groups that were mixed ages and levels of competence. At Hogadon, they had a dedicated slope for the beginners. This allowed them to separate students into smaller groups. This, in turn, encouraged more skiers to become instructors since they could specialize in teaching one ability group. Also, it

helped get the parents skiing because they brought their kids up and then stayed to learn.[13]

According to Glenn Bochmann, the first head of the ski school was Barry Corbet, who came from Jackson. Bob Kidd felt that Corbet was one of the best NCAA Division One skiers in the West. He brought great skiing techniques and an ability to teach. Bob thought he learned much that later gave him an edge from Corbet. Corbet stayed a season and then moved back to Jackson and bought a hotel at the bottom of the Snow King chairlift.[14]

Drew Jensen, also from Jackson, arrived to take over. Both he and Corbet were there during the pre-opening planning stages. When Hogadon finally opened during the 1959–60 ski season, it became obvious that they needed someone to run the school on a regular basis. For the 1959–60 season, they hired Jack Cowan, who was from Casper and a second-generation mountain skier. His father, Frank, was the mayor in the 1920s. Frank was friends with Cy Bon and skied with him and Nils Fougstedt in the 1920s. Jack Cowan was also the ski area manager.[15]

When Jack decided to narrow his work down to his ski shop and to his National Ski Patrol, Northern Division duties, the CMSC began looking for a new head of the ski school. Ken Barnes came from Colorado as a geologist with the Humble Oil Company. He had gotten certified as a ski instructor while living down there. Bill Garberg remembered that Bill Haines, Glenn Bochmann, Pat Burgess, Marilyn Ladd, and he all continued to teach when Ken Barnes became the third director to run the program.[16] All of the instructors got their certification in the next three or four years.[17]

Since all of the ski school directors were part-time, this was perfect for a man with another job. Ken had been part of the team that had organized the ski instructors on Nursery. All of them transferred over when Hogadon opened. Shortly after that, Ken's job transferred him out, leaving another hole in leadership. Bill Garberg and Glenn Bochmann jointly took over as directors until 1962, when Glenn also stepped down. The Casper Mountain Ski Corporation hired

Top: **These are some of the early ski instructors. From the left: Don Burgess, Angus Morrison, Isabel Perry, Don Perry, Pat Burgess, and Marilyn Ladd.** *(Glenn Bochmann collection)* Bottom: **This plaque shows the Hogadon ski instructors in the late 1960s.**

Bill Garberg as their newest ski school director. Bill remembered that he did that job until the 1987–88 season ended.[18] Then, Kenny Bale started and ran the program until 2009.[19] The director of the Ski School in 2019 was Dave LaPlante.[20]

Garberg recalled that within a year or so, they had around a hundred students, mostly kids. Around thirty-two instructors taught every class, every week, during the ski season. The busiest—and most financially profitable—week was between Christmas and New Year's Eve, when everyone had new ski equipment that they wanted to learn how to use.[21]

Some years were problematic. Bill Garberg described a problem related to snow cover. "We always seemed to have enough snow to get by except for one year. Then I remember

Pat Burgess is training ski instructors. *(Glenn Bochmann collection)*

that first year that they put the chairlift in. I went and bought $8,000 worth of advertising for the area and gave one ski lesson that year. We had no snow, absolutely no snow."[22]

The ski school instructors had special coats they wore. According to Bruce Ladd, his dad (Bill) and Don Perry designed them.

> Well, some of the other interviewees might remember this, but it was almost like we were trying to make fun of them, but the spouses were— but the ski school was so proud of their first jackets. They were kind of a light brown with a little bit of gold trim on the sleeve. So, my dad and Don Perry were instrumental in making these kind— they would go down to the army surplus and got these major's jackets that was kind of a dark brown. And they put a yellow band on, and they got their names embroidered on them. And I don't know where this name ever came from, but they were the Monksters. But they were obviously meant to make fun of the ski school.[23]

Instructor training was vital to training the students. Marilyn Ladd, in her 2014 Casper Ski History Project oral history interview, commented on how they trained new instructor recruits.

> Weaver: You were a ski instructor for how long?
> Marilyn: For about twenty-five years. Oh, my goodness. Let's see. Probably started in early '60s.
> Bill: You know, I think you actually started your clinicing on Nursery though, before Hogadon was operational.
> Marilyn: Well, we just did that because you could get to it.
> Weaver: Did you just walk up or— the [portable] tow was gone by that time.
> Marilyn: We would do dryland training in a park somewhere downtown and learned all these little tricks of the trade. At that time, our youngest child, Leanne, was a baby, and I would sit her out in the middle and then we'd walk around the outside. Leanne's in her fifties now.[24]

Garberg laid out a typical day of training ski school instructors. This started under Ken Barnes, and then Garberg led the training. New instructors started by coming to his house, and

Top: **Pat Burgess leading the pack** *(Photograph by Glenn Bochmann)* Right: **Happy ski students in line for the tow** *(Photograph by Glenn Bochmann)*

he took them through the manual, which was thirty-eight pages long. Garberg wrote it, and then he and some of the women lithographed it and put the copies together. Bill took the manual to a Northern Division meeting, and they were so impressed that they asked for a copy to use to train a broader group of instructors. The Northern Division trainers used it for many years.[25]

Before Garberg began the formal training at Hogadon, his ski instructors went up to Montana, usually to Bozeman or Red Lodge, or to Snowbird, Utah. They trained with members of other groups, sometimes eighty to ninety instructors from all over the United States. The trainings were ten days long, with two days of going through the ski techniques. Garberg described the dominant technique as the American method that came out of the Austrian or French *circulaire*. That technique emphasized the idea that the upper body did very little and that it was all about knees, feet, and hips. He said it was still like that: "Keep the upper body as quiet as you can."[26]

Early on at Hogadon, the instructors started the day packing the beginner slope. There were two class times. The first was from 9:00 a.m. to 12:00 p.m. and the second was from 1:00 p.m. to 3:00 p.m.[27] The lessons ran for five to six weeks, and the kids got a completion medal when they graduated.[28]

Bill Garberg figured he probably gave over twenty thousand lessons over the twenty years he taught. The corporation and the city had a deal through which the families could buy a lift ticket and a series of lessons for a package rate. He got a discount on the lift tickets, so he got a lot of students. That was still continuing in 2016.[29]

Elementary School Ski Days

Diane Neste contacted Sandy Leotta to share a memory she had about a skiing opportunity she was involved with creating in the 1980s.

> I started the Kinderski program through ski school when our son Kirk started kindergarten in 1987. It was held in the afternoon once a week after morning kindergarten. My good friend Sue Johnson helped me set it up. I think the program went for about four years. At its height, we had about fifty kids in the program. We would often drive to kids' houses to pick them up and then delivered them back home again. I know by the time the kids were in high school, almost every boy skiing on the NC [Natrona County] team had started in Kinderski. We provided all our own teaching aids, including carpet and buttons. There are still a few Diane's Dynamo buttons floating around.[30]

Another elementary school program came into existence in the twenty-first century. Gary Vantrease, Hogadon manager, and Chris Smith, the director of the ski school, worked out a joint agreement with the Natrona County School District to develop a physical education component that got fifth graders up on the slopes to ski. The program eventually included students from other districts, with students coming from as far as Wheatland, a hundred miles away. The students got a two- to three-hour lesson, equipment rental, and a tow ticket for $25 per day. The ski area picked up the cost for low-income students.[31] It was still running in 2019.[32]

Hogadon Snow Sports students take a lesson *(Hogadon Basin Ski Area collection)*

Alpine Racing

Many of the people interviewed for the ski history project noted that although Casper Mountain did not have the longest or toughest hills around, the combination of snow, challenging smaller slopes, and great teaching led to skiers who went on to become experts. Casper turned out many good racers, some of whom went on to race in college and beyond.

Barry Horn was one of many Casper skiers who raced for the University of Colorado (CU) Boulder team. Quite a few raced for Denver University. Others, like Bob Kidd, skied for the University of Wyoming. Bob went to university on a National College Athletic Association (NCAA) ski scholarship. Bob had made the Northern Division Junior National Ski Team in high school. That team won three times. Once he was in college, his team won the NCAA Division One championship in skiing. In 2007, Bob Kidd was named to the University of Wyoming Athletic Hall of Fame with his 1968 teammates.

Angie Morrison felt that the racing spirit not only led to winning local races but, eventually, to many of the racers coming back to teach the next generation. He said,

> Then we moved all that from there [Nursery] over to Hogadon, and we continue that today with the Casper Mountain Racers. It made a big improvement. Bobby Kidd is one of them; he's still one of our coaches. We've gone through a number of coaches over the years. Casper has always shone in competition within this Northern Division. There's nine divisions in the United States. Casper is in the Northern Division. And our kids here have always placed in the higher part of these competitions. Even some of the kids that went through our programs on the old Nursery in early days, they ended up being coaches in our ski school. So that's how it came about.[33]

Barry Horn, who began racing on Miner and Spillway, described the lure of racing.

> Weaver: What about racing? You were a racer. Tell us about that.
>
> Horn: Well, just kind of fell into that. Just started—everything we did was competition. Any time you went skiing, you were competing with your friends and whoever was next to you and everything else, trying to be a little bit better, little bit faster, a little fancier.
>
> Weaver: How did you guys get new techniques coming in, to improve your skiing?
>
> Horn: Well, we saw a lot of stuff in films, like newsreels. I think there was educational, learn-to-ski type films. They'd show you the new techniques when they came out with new stuff. Parallel technique and when the French technique came out, you watched how and you studied how they did that. You read it. They used to have in magazines, ski magazines, they would have all that stuff. They would describe how it's done. And you'd go out and do it, trial and error.
>
> Weaver: Were there older skiers that would bring in new things and show you guys?
>
> Horn: Yeah. I remember Mike Leon. He came up and he had some French skis, the newest thing. Vampires. Had Vampire skis and they were really long. Probably 220s. With the French long thongs. The first time we'd seen small toe irons and the long French thong. Of course, that's what we all used after that. We used those leg breakers. But they were good because you had absolute control. The ski was really part of your foot. We learned a lot of the French technique from Mike. I think he'd picked it up in Europe.
>
> The early races were run by Chuck Morrison, Rob Robertson, and Buck Weaver.[34]

Barry Horn described packing the snow by strapping on skis and side stepping upwards on the slopes to reduce the ruts made by previous skiers. This gave the racers time to gauge the terrain and plan their race strategies for that day.[35] They also poured salt on the snow to help stabilize it and put food coloring on the holes where the poles went. That way, they could replace them if they came out.[36]

Horn also recalled that the main race hills in the late forties (and until Hogadon opened) were Miner and Spillway. Here is his description of racing on Spillway.

> Horn: The downhill was Spillway. They did set a few control gates on Spillway, but it was more for safety than it was for technical reasons, trying to keep you out of the trees, basically.
>
> Weaver: You couldn't cut through the zigzags, right?
>
> Horn: The zigzags? No, you couldn't cut through them. Actually, I don't think you'd make it if you tried that. That's what the little gates were for is to keep you out of the trees. It was much just a zigzag thing. Until the bottom, and then that was just a long glide on a sidehill—a sidehill that made it a little tricky.[37]

Hogadon Basin Invitational Giant Slalom Race

A few months after it opened in February 1960, the Casper Mountain Ski Club organized the Hogadon Basin Invitational Giant Slalom Race. The race was open to members of the Casper Mountain Ski Club and both the northern regional and national ski associations. Held on Sunday, February 21, it had classifications for expert, intermediate, and novice adults and categories for young skiers between the ages of eight and eighteen.

The winners of the categories were as follows. In the Junior Boys category, Billy Kidd was first, Kent Flower was second, and Arnold Ferrin came in third. The Men's B category was led by Jack Cowan, with Barry Horn second. In the Men's C category, first place went to Eddie Summerford,

with Dick Schirk in second and Bill Mallick in third. For the women, Marge Speas, followed by Ann Cowan and then Pat Burgess were the three top skiers for the Women's division. The Junior Girls division featured Karen Korfonte in first, Debbie Davis in second, and Janet Swann took third place. The Under Nine category had Jay Cowan in first, followed by Nicky Garberg and David Chism.[38]

The Can-Am Race

Glenn Bochmann remembered the race.

> Then we had a Can-Am meet here one time. That was 1972. They had people that were world-class skiers come here; it was one of the training deals for people who were in the Olympics. They had people here from Canada and all over that were training in other places.
>
> Tom Stroock was the big gun on that one. He just wanted to get a big ski race in Casper. At the time, there were rules that there had to be, for a slalom race, there had to be so much vertical drop. So, they said this hill had to have a 610-foot vertical on it. So, we built a ramp up onto the side of the warming hut. They'd start the race up there on top and come down. Then they'd go through about where that starting gate is now. We found out later that you didn't have to have that 610 feet. Six hundred was fine. So, we finally tore that thing down. Got quite a thrill coming off that building on that sharp a drop because it was just like it bottomed you out when you hit the bottom.
>
> But that could have been such a good race. But we had a ferocious snowstorm that weekend. It was just— the city came together and really went all out to put on a good race. And it was a good race. It really went well. But I remember that storm. The National Guard put up tents and the highway made sure that the roads were clear.

This is the side view of the first Hogadon Lodge. They built a ramp for the Can-Am Race off of the roof. *(Bob Hardesty collection)*

But the hill just wasn't all that good. But that snowstorm was just unbelievable. You can talk to some of the people in town because they had a lot of [interest in the race]. Some of the top racers in the United States plus the Canadians. It was a good race. Went off well.

I remember that. That structure was up on the front of the warming hut for years, and they finally took it down. In fact, they used it one year for a city ski race. But you had to shovel all the snow up on the ramp. There used to be a staircase. Because it was going to be an observation up on top there. There was a deck thing that went up on the east side of the building, set of stairs to the top. I went off of there once, but only once. It would really get you started because they used to hold the downhill on Park Avenue. And they'd go down through that slot and hit the face of Park. There were some wild downhills, I'll tell you.

And it's probably a good thing that that stopped because that's a bunny hill now or beginner's hill. This was usually held late enough in the year that there weren't any beginners up there. That had some good jumps on that.[39]

Sandy Leotta shared some of her memories of the race. "The CanAm (FIS race) race brought in teams from around the world. They were impressed at the friendliness of Casper residents. One team set up in a garage, prepping their equipment. The owner came out and offered them cocoa. Then they found out they were in the wrong house, but the folks were still nice."[40]

The following is from Marilyn and Bill Ladd.

Bill: The Canadian ski team and the United States ski team. A lot of those skiers went on to ski in the Olympics.

Sandy: When they timed the races in the 1960s, the person at the top waved a bamboo pole and the person at the bottom turned on a stopwatch. In the 1970s, they got electric timing gear. [She remembered that Sam Hake, an electrical engineer at the University of Wyoming, invented the system.][41]

Marilyn: But Bill was so cautious and careful to do everything as he was told. And he's an engineer, so he did it very methodically. It just so happened that they had a tent at the bottom of the hill where the timing hut was. I don't know who was in there as the timer. But Bill didn't want anyone else in there because it was pretty important that the time be recorded accurately.

So, he walked up the hill, he was behind a person, he went in and said, "Get out of here." Turned out it was the governor of the state of Wyoming!

Bill: But he got out.[42]

The Casper Race

Warren Weaver was the chairman of the February 16, 1958, City Ski Meet. It consisted of both downhill and slalom races. The prize for the best skier was the Kistler trophy, donated by Lou Kistler of Kistler Sporting Goods. It was a traveling trophy, but the competitor who won it three times got to keep it.[43]

A week after the City Race, there was also a state invitational race on February 25 and 26, 1958. This race in Jackson Hole, Wyoming, featured the Natrona County High School (NCHS) team. The members included Dick Armstrong, Bruce Cody, Bill Kidd, Bob Sensentaffer, and Ed Summerford. Their coach was Bill Mallick. They were competing against teams from Colorado, Utah, Idaho, and Montana. There was a follow-up race featuring giant slalom and jumping held from March 22 to March 23, 1958.[44] It was a busy season for the NCHS team.

Many oral histories and newspaper articles covered the City Ski Meets. The March 30, 1967, issue of the *Casper Star-Tribune* talked about that coming weekend's 1967 annual race. It contained a picture of Bob Hardesty, Hogadon manager, and Dr. Oda Sully, president of the Casper Mountain Ski Club, holding the trophies for the race. It also included a list of the winners from the race's origin in 1948.[45]

Race chairman Buck Weaver has racers draw starting numbers in 1955. *(Fred Walters collection)*

1948 – Arthur French	1949 – Bill Johnston
1950 – Bob Hardesty	1951 – Bob Hardesty
1952 – Bob Nussbaum	1953 – Bob Hardesty
1954 – Bob Hardesty	1955 – Vic Poirier

1956 – Vic Poirier	1957 – Lew Penwell
1958 – Dick Schirk	1959 – Barry Horn
1960 – Jack Cowan	1961 – Ed Summerford
1962 – Henry Phibbs	1963 – Bob Kidd
1964 – Ed Summerford	1965 – Bruce Studer
1966 – Bob Kidd	

The City Champion First Place Women's Cup was first presented in 1961. Glenn and Chris Bochmann donated it through their Skier Shop. The winners and their years were as follows.

1961 – Ann Cowan	1962 – Susy Studer
1963 – Susy Studer	1964 – Judy Snedden
1965 – Sofie Aarheim	1966 – Sandy Stroock
1967 – Sandy Stroock	1968 – Kathy Garberg

Top: **In the February 1992 Casper Classic, this team of women ski patrollers called themselves Team Fear. They were Jan Chambers, MaryAnn Hoff, Debbie Huber, and Chris Muth.** *(Photograph by Gay Nations)* Right: **Bob and Phyllis Hardesty show off their trophies after winning the Senior division of the City Race.** *(Photograph by Glenn Bochmann)*

Many of the older skiers continued to race and win. Some senior teams were made up of groups of friends who kept up a friendly competition over the years. Jan Chambers was part of a ski patrol team that competed in the City Race. She teamed up with MaryAnn Hoff, Debbie Huber, and Chris Muth to ski as Team Fear.

High School-Age Club Racing

Soon, there were enough budding racers that Hogadon management decided to hire a dedicated racing coach. In 1969, the Casper Mountain Ski Club hired Jim Weiss from Montana. Weiss coached until the early 1980s. He taught

the advanced skiers.[46] Bruce Lamberson recalled that Weiss was the first teacher to come along who could begin to teach them world-class technique.[47]

Jim brought his wife, Jean, with him when he came to Casper. She was also a top-notch instructor, but she was overshadowed by Jim. Eventually, the couple divorced, and Jean went to Vail and became one of their premier ski instructors. They were part of an international association of ski instructors called Interski.[48] Jim later married Diana Vincent, who also shared his love of skiing. Later, Jim became a rancher in Idaho.[49]

Weiss developed an interest in skiing as a teen, but he spent time in college and in the US Air Force before he moved to Whitefish, Montana, and became a ski coach. He worked for K2 and Rossignol as a ski coach for the 1972 US Olympic team. He also helped create the Professional Ski Instructors Association (PSIA). He skied in almost every country that had ski mountains.[50]

Jim Weiss had worked at Whitefish, Montana, before he got hired at Hogadon. He had also been an examiner to certify new ski instructors in the Northern Division. The Casper Mountain Ski Club had been running the ski school, and they realized that their young racers needed better training. According to Bruce Ladd, this was after taking some of the CMSC members to a meet in Whitefish. Those members included Sandy and Grace Stroock. According to Tom Stroock, the CMSC brought Weiss on in early 1969, and he soon had the program going at full speed.[51]

Weiss devised a plan to divide up the teaching, working with his wife, Jean, Glenn Bochmann, and Bill Haines. Each one took a group (level) of skiers. They had bibs over their ski clothes. Jim taught advanced

Jim Weiss was an early Casper Mountain Racers coach. *(Weiss family collection)*

students, who wore red bibs; Bills' group wore yellow bibs; and Glenn's group were less experienced and formed the lower-middle group, who wore blue bibs. Bruce Ladd started out in Glenn's group. Jean Weiss had the youngest kids with the least experience. They wore green bibs.[52]

Sandy Leotta gave us more insight into Jim Weiss. "He made a big difference in ski techniques of all the instructors and racers he coached, as he was a master ski technician. What a difference he made in my life, and what an ornery, loveable character he was."[53] According to Bruce Ladd, racing, especially older kids racing, was a natural outgrowth of the ski school. This was especially true from the time that Jim Weiss came on the scene.[54]

In the 1950s, there was not a formal, sanctioned high school ski team. It was an extracurricular activity. Chuck Morrison was an early leader in the effort to get a high school team going. The Casper Mountain Ski Club had their own high school-age team until around 1960, which they helped fund. Then after that, they still helped out and continued to give them access to the Ski Team Slope at Hogadon.[55]

Their coach was Bill Haines. Anker Larson, who was a teacher at Natrona County High School, worked with Haines to get the racers to overnight meets across Wyoming. According to Bruce Ladd, Larson conscripted other skiers to help with the team. He remembered that Bill Haines and Glenn Bochmann were willing recruits.[56]

Sandy Stroock (Leotta) was skiing a lot at Hogadon when she was in ninth grade. She was on the Hogadon ski team,

Anker Larson and Bill Haines take a run at Hogadon in 1968. *(Photograph by Glenn Bochmann)*

The Natrona County High School team was ready for the Wyoming High School Ski Meet in 1968. *(Photograph by Leon Campbell)*

which included Bob and Lynn Frost, Judy Sneddon, and Susie and Bruce Studer. Sandy noted additional teammates as follows.

> But then when I was in ninth grade, the older guys were like Brian Hubley, Robbie Bryans, Denny West, Cam Walker, Monte Robertson. Andy Ayres was only a year ahead of me, I think. Dale and Steve Popish. Judy Sulley. Dr. Sulley was a very well-loved doctor. When he passed away, Sulley's Run is named after him. His kids were Mike and Judy, Kevin and Carol. And they were all really good skiers. Judy was just a year ahead of me. She and Marla Speas, now Wold, were the older women on the team. I skied with Grace Robertson and Kathy Garberg and Althea Burgess. Anker, Glenn Bochmann, and Bill Haines helped the kids run gates. They traveled to meets with Bob Kidd or, later, Anker Larsen.[57]

Leotta described moving up to the Natrona County High School's club team.

> The high school ski team was great fun. We trained together at Hogadon, the older kids helping the younger ones. There were two circuits of races. One was the high school races all over the state, and the other was the FIS [International Federation of Ski] races, where race results gave you points on an international system. The idea was to get low points by racing against lower point and better racers. There was friction between these two circuits because to win the state races, the team needed the FIS racers and often, the races were on the same weekends. We traveled together to races all over Montana and Wyoming. Often, we had adults take us. Rob Robertson once flew us to Kalispell,

Montana, in his plane, and we got stuck there with bad weather. Sometimes, we'd travel on our own. I remember driving home from Kalispell once, going home to shower and change clothes, and then going to school. I fell asleep sitting in English class as my head fell off my propped-up hand. In Montana, we usually were housed in the homes of our competitors. We would show up to a race in Montana and be envious of the teams with coaches and ski uniforms. Anker and Bill Haines and sometimes parents like Mary West drove us on [trips to] high school races.[58]

Cam Walker did not get to ski on the NCHS team until he was a senior. His mother thought poorly of the kids who raced, and she did not want her son to get distracted from his academics. But when he was a senior, she relented. He remembered that was the year that Casper beat Jackson. He felt that his teammates were some of the best skiers in the state. They included Brian Hubley, Monte Robertson, Denny West, Emrick Huber, Bruce Studer, and Robby Bryans. Anker Larsen was still the team sponsor that year.[59]

During the oral history with Chris Smith, Sandy Leotta asked him a question.

> Sandy: I wanted to ask—drastically changing topics— but we haven't talked much about the high school ski racers because your wife, Christy, coached downhill racers. What's their role on the hill?
>
> Chris: They've actually gotten really good. John Miller, he's the coach for NC, and John's a former CMR [Casper Mountain Racers] kid. He raced at Rocky Mountain College. John is a third- or fourth-grade teacher in the NC District. Had a championship kids' soccer team this year. That was kinda cool.
>
> Jim's come back. He coaches the NC team. And he coaches a lot of the KW [Kelly Walsh

High School] team because Ben Schirk, who was a former tennis teacher— I don't know how Ben got talked into this, but he's a great guy. We've actually even got him to ski—not very well, but he does ski.

> But the kids love him. And he's a good recruiter. Even when Christy did the school, the hard part was she wasn't a teacher in the schools, so it's hard to reach the kids. Where Ben, he'll see a kid walking down the hall and say, "Hey, what're you doing? Wouldn't you like to be on the ski team? Free trips to go to ski areas."
>
> He's a good recruiter. And he and John have grown that program. I'd say four years ago, I thought the team was going to fold. It just wasn't enough. Tommy Ellbogen had been the coach forever. He'd gotten tired of it and wanted to move on. My wife had gotten tired of it. She had enough and she left. But John's doing a great job. He's a good coach. Ben's a great recruiter. I think they're very good advocates for the high school program.[60]

Bruce Ladd was a racer from the time he was six. Since his mom was an instructor, he could travel to clinics and races. He started in the midget category, gradually moving up to novice 1 and 2, to intermediate, and, eventually, to expert. He had the opportunity to participate in a lot of Wyoming and Montana Northern Division races. When he moved up to become a high school racer, he actually started out in middle school. The way he told it was as follows.

> Actually, high school back then was grades ten, eleven and twelve. My first opportunity to race high school was in ninth grade because I was at home and the gang—that was Roger Bochmann and Chuck Bromley and Russell Horstman—they were all a few years older than me. They were down there in Laramie at the

Casper Junior College ski club members hike from the college toward the mountain as they get into shape to ski. *(Photograph by Bob Hardesty)*

state meet with Anker [Larson], and they went out and had pizza and got food poisoning. They were all up in the hotel room, just sick as a dog. Anker called my parents up and said, "Is there any way Bruce could get down here because I don't have a team?" Dad said, "Well, Bruce is only in ninth grade. He's going to CY [Junior High School]." Anker said, "Well, I'll get him in somehow." So, I went down to the bus depot with my skis, about 7:30 at night. And there was a bus to Cheyenne. I waited 'til about two in the morning, and then there was a bus over to Laramie. Then I carried my skis to the hotel and knocked on Anker's door. He had a spare bed for me, and then I ski raced, and I was the only NC racer. So, I started high school racing in ninth grade.[61]

College

Arthur French skied on the Casper College team. The Casper College team was organized informally in the fall of 1948. It was sponsored by the Casper Junior College Ski Association. Dick Perkins was the president, and its members were Skip Curry, Carol Gutz, Leaver Briggs, and Alvin and Bob McAllister. Chuck Morrison was the sponsor. The group worked on widening and improving Miner Run and improving and expanding cross-country trails. They also were organizing a ski patrol.[62] According to the college paper *The Chinook*, the club was struggling to get a team going. The November 16, 1951, issue documented club meetings and training sessions.[63]

Casper Mountain Racers (CMR)

The Casper Mountain Racers were a project of the Casper Mountain Ski Club. They started as a dedicated team around 1969.[64] Like the other ski school programs, the CMR began as an ad hoc endeavor and then gradually professionalized.

Early program directors also served as heads of the ski school. This continued even after Hogadon began to have professional paid directors. From 1972 to 1975, Glenn Bochmann coached the Racers.[65] When Bob Kidd moved back from Sublette County, he and Bruce Studer talked with Joe Koenig, who was the president of the CMR. Both of them wanted their kids in the Racers. Koenig wanted Bob and Bruce to coach the teams. They agreed, but they committed to always teach for free. Bob and Bruce coached together until Bruce's death in 2003. Bob continues to teach to this day. He has been there for the team for thirty years.[66]

When Sandy Stroock was just out of high school, she went to Argentina to work in San Martín de los Andes, Argentina. Not only did she teach skiing but she also met her future husband, Miguel Leotta. Sandy noted, "In the late '90s, through 2002, when our two daughters were skiing in high school, the Casper ski club needed a coach and we hired Mario Alvarez from San Martín, a good friend of ours from Miguel's hometown. He coached the Casper ski club for five years and took a few of the skiers to San Martín to train during our summers. These skiers were Maria Leotta, Pat Moran, Aaron Dahill, Jena Akin, Alex Martin, Adam Studer, and others."[67]

Chris Weaver, a member of the Racers during that time, was also one of the teens who went on a San Martín trip. Chris, as well as his brother Sam and sister Cara, participated in the CMR. Their mother, Laurie Weaver, taught in the Racers and was a key board member and fund raiser.[68]

This was the Casper Mountain Racers team in 1972–73. *(Photograph by Glenn Bochmann)*

In 1978, Laurie Marancik came to Wyoming from New York after a period of time spent teaching skiing at the ski area outside of Red Lodge, Montana. She had followed her brothers John and Pete there and then followed them to Casper. Her brothers had become friends with Sara and Warren Weaver and their sons Sam and Tim. That led to her becoming a ski instructor at Hogadon in 1979. She remembered beginning her ski instructor training in December that year. She soon fell in love with Sam Weaver, and they married in 1983. They had three kids. When Laurie started teaching skiing, Bill Garberg was running the program. Her co-instructors were Glenn and Pat Bochmann, Mary Lou and Angus Morrison, Bob and Phyllis Hardesty, and Bill Haines. Of course, there were others as well, but these people became her friends. They were people who had also been friends of Warren and Sara Weaver. As it so often happened in the ski community, this was a cross-generational friendship.[69]

Laurie began to get involved in the Casper Mountain Racers when her oldest son, Sam, was young. That was around 1989. She was then a Casper Mountain Racers instructor until her youngest child, Cara, stopped racing around 2000.[70]

This is the 2020 swap meet fundraiser for the Casper Mountain Racers.

When Laurie started helping with the CMR, the coach was Bob Murphy. He coached while young Sam was racing. After that, they imported Mario from Argentina and someone from France. Mario stayed the longest.[71] Especially after Chris Weaver joined the CMR, Laurie was on the board. For several years, she received the volunteer-of-the-year award. She organized their signature fundraising event, the Black Tie and Levi Banquet and silent auction. They also had a big ski swap.

One of the things that Laurie and most of the other participants in the oral history interviews noted was that the ski instructors and the ski patrol formed two distinct groups. Often, one spouse was in one group and one was in the other group. The volunteer opportunities were many, and that allowed for people to find the best way to use their talents.

Chris Smith came from the East and moved to Casper in 2007 to lead the Casper Mountain Racers program. He credits Bob Kidd with getting him to come here. Smith had spent his time as a professional coach before coming to Casper. He wanted to settle down and buy a house, which he could afford to do in Casper.[72] He coached for the Casper Mountain Racers from 2007 to 2013. By 2013, he was tired of coaching and wanted a new challenge. His wife, Christy, worked in the schools and had helped coach the high school ski team. Chris is very focused on pro-level racing. The programs Chris was very proud of were the racing program and the elementary program he and Gary Vantrease had put together with Natrona County School District.[73]

The Casper Mountain Racers website in 2021 describes the programs they offer. They have a fee structure to participate. The Kidd-Studer Program is for skiers ages five to twelve who know how to ski but are still novices. The Alpine Ski Team is for advanced students aged ten to sixteen. They ski in US Ski and Snowboard Association (USSA) races if they have a

This ski patrol badge belonged to Warren (Buck) Weaver. *(Weaver-Hunt collection)*

competition license. There is also a High School Home Team for skiers at NCHS and Kelly Walsh High School (KWHS). The fee was $750.

The Ski Patrol

The Origins of the National Ski Patrol (NSP)

In the early 1930s, the president of the National Ski Association, Roger F. Langley, proposed that the association form a committee on ski safety and training. The model he looked at was the Mt. Mansfield Ski Patrol at Stowe, Vermont. The founder of the Mansfield patrol and future founder of the 10th Mountain Division was Charles Minot "Minnie" Dole.[74] He and Langley formed the committee that, in 1938, became the National Ski Patrol (NSP). Dole made Langley NSP member #1.[75] Dole was the director of the NSP until 1950.

The NSP formed the Rocky Mountain Division in February of 1938, signaling that the western United States was becoming the prime area of the country for skiing. One of the earliest members of the NSP was the Loveland Ski area in Colorado. Minnie Dole noted in 1938 that "we all know that accidents happen in skiing as in any other sport, but we also know that they

The National Ski Patrol System Manual from 1941 (Susan Bishop collection)

can be greatly reduced by a commonsense attitude toward the sport and through widespread education by facts."[76]

The National Ski Patrol has set standards for safety and training and is the arbiter for who is qualified to be on a ski patrol. They provide training from beginner to advanced patroller and, over the years, have expanded their training to include mountain biking and both Alpine and Nordic skiing. They believe their ski patrol responsibility code should be the rule all outdoor enthusiasts follow.

Ski Patrol on Casper Mountain

An article in the January 17, 1964, *Casper Star-Tribune* noted that there had been informal ski patrols on the mountain since 1933. In 1958, the *Casper Tribune-Herald* said the following: "A well-organized ski patrol, under the direction of Dick Armstrong, is operating on the mountain. If you have had any training in first aid and are a competent skier, you may wish to work with the patrol. If interested, please call Dick."[77]

The Casper ski patrol grew along with the mountain's ski slopes and facilities. The 1964 article gave additional details, noting that there were forty-three members in the patrol at the time. It listed the members and also noted that the patrol had been affiliated with the National Ski Patrol since 1959.[78]

Membership in the ski patrol required long hours of training, and they also agreed to many hours of patrolling and many more hours of refresher training. In return, members built a sense of contributing to fellow skiers and satisfaction from developing their own skills. They also built a network of dear friends whom they patrolled with several times a month and met at social gatherings and monthly patrol meetings. Many also traveled to out-of-town Northern Division trainings and meetings. This went on for years, with many devoting fifty years to ski patrolling. One long-term member who received a fifty-year award was Sean Ellis, who started as a junior patroller. Other fifty-year or more members were Bill Chambers, Jan Chambers, MaryAnn Hoff, Mike Huber, and Kent Doing.

Top: Bill Maires had been a patroller for more than thirty years when he took this last pre-retirement run in 2012. (*Photograph courtesy of* Casper Star-Tribune)
Right: Bill, Jan, and Will Chambers take a break on a patrol day. (*Photograph by Gay Nations*)

The junior patrol program was a major asset to ensure the continued existence of the program. MaryAnn Hoff says it best.

The Junior Ski Patrol Program has been an import ant part of the patrol and has given young folks or children of patrollers a chance to serve on the patrol until they old enough to be regular patrollers. Many of the leaders in the patrol began as junior patrollers. Duties include helping patrollers on accidents and on the hill and in the hut, putting up ropes, fences, learning medical skills, and of course they had to keep the wood box full for the A-frame and eat up the extra food crews would always have available! Some of the junior patrollers became leaders on the patrol. To mention a few, Sean Ellis, Mike Huber, Sam Weaver (late), Tim Weaver, Kent Doing continued to serve on the patrol in leadership roles. Many have been patrolling for decades, with children and grandchildren following their example. It continues to be generational, and the ski patrollers have a special bond in their love of skiing and desire to be of service.[79]

Leadership took many forms. Some gravitated to first aid and safety training. Others became organizational leaders, doing less visible jobs. One such key person on the Casper Mountain Ski Patrol (CMSP) was Stan Lowe (late), known as our

Top: **Helen Schilling, Gay Nations, and Stan Lowe in the patrol building.** (*Photograph by Gay Nations*) Bottom: This is Crew B (Saturday ski patrol crew) about 2010. It shows the multigenerational nature of the patrol. Top, left to right: Cassady Hoff, Kavin Hoff, Kevin Hoff, Arik Christenson, Bill Bays, Pat Harshman, and Ken Hoff; bottom, let to right: Rogen Hoff, Kyle Christensen, Bill Maires, and MaryAnn Hoff. (*Photograph by Gay Nations*)

"Legal Begal." Stan was our legal representative, and he made sure our bylaws and operating procedures were up to date and covered legal aspects of patrolling in regard to liability. He was also the Northern Division legal advisor, and Stan's influence reached the national level, writing the Ski Patrol Responsibility Code.[80]

The February/March 1980 issue of *Casper Magazine* featured a story on the Casper Mountain Ski Patrol. The author called them "The Masked Cavaliers" and documented the daily work of a patroller, but he also looked at their training.

The author also included the local patrol's history. It said that in the 1930s, shortly after the National Ski Patrol started, Casper skiers met to set up their own group. The author credited Buck Weaver, Gay Nations, Don Burgess, and Bob Hardesty with being the organizers.[81] Angus Morrison noted that others included Lou Demorest and Dr. Brendan Phibbs. Quite a few of the early members had been in Boy Scouts Troop #9 over the years.[82] In his 2016 interview, Charlie Peak said that he thought his dad, George, and Howie Bronsdon had a part in creating the Casper Mountain Ski Patrol.[83]

According to Angus Morrison, the ski patrol dated to the days when Nursery was still the only ski slope. Morrison recalled that Buck Weaver, who used an old toboggan to rescue injured skiers, began to organize other skiers to help with rescues.[84] Angie described the toboggan and an early rescue in the following way.

> Anybody got hurt on the hill, we had an old toboggan that looked like the beavers had ate the front of it off. We'd get a bunch of people and carry the people down to put them on the sled, and then take them down to the vehicles and take them to the hospital.
>
> I remember one time, this woman broke her leg in about six places. She wanted to ski, so somebody

Above: **This World War II surplus *aukial* was the most common type of rescue sled used in the early days of the ski patrol. A note on wording: Many of the old timers called a toboggan by a word that sounded like *aukial*, which was, in fact, *ahkio*, a Finnish word for toboggan. It was a word brought over from Sweden by Nils and Ole Fougstedt, but it was also a term used by the Norwegian troops who trained with the World War II 10th Mountain Division skiers.** Left: New-generation toboggans *(Gay Nations collection)*

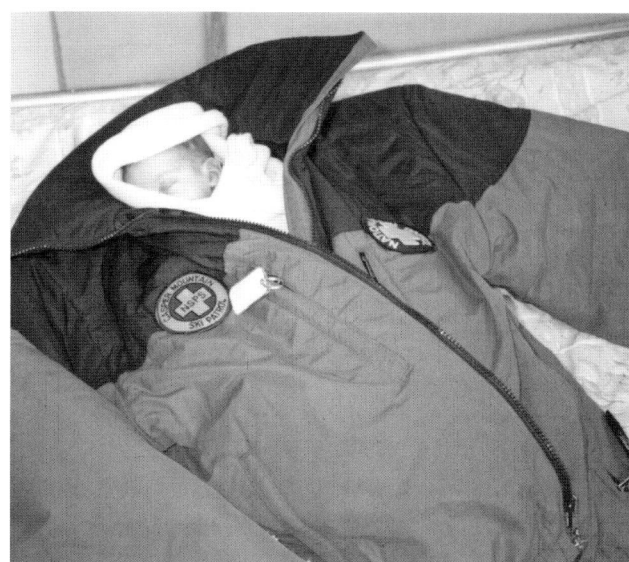

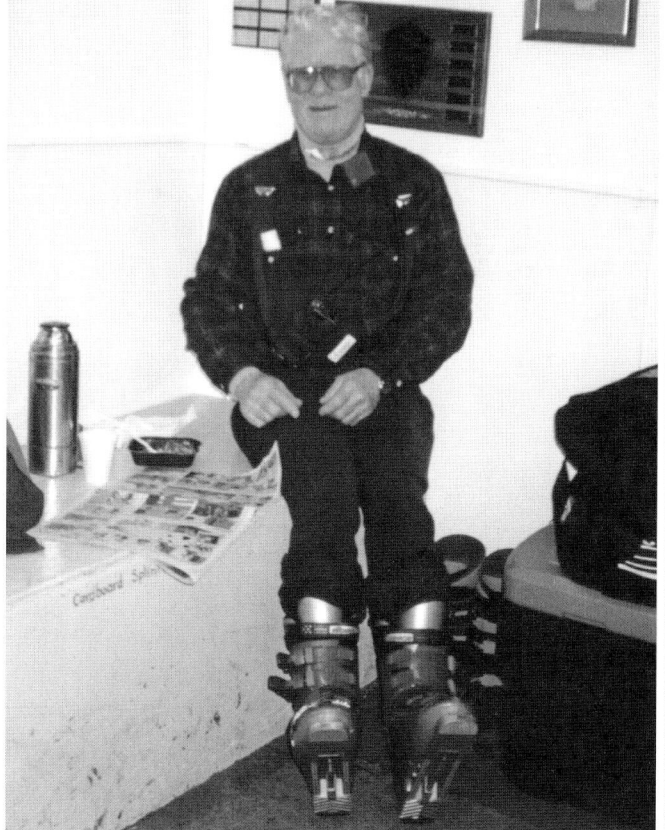

Clockwise from top

Toboggan training *(Gay Nations collection)*; Pinky Ellis waits for a call in the new patrol building. *(Photograph by Gay Nations)*; This ski patrol jacket is an impromptu bed for a potential future patroller. *(Photograph by Gay Nations)*

stood her on a pair of skis. She had these regular street shoes on, just barely going and fell and broke her leg in six places, we found out later. Buck come down with the sled and said we'll put her on here. But we got to carry her down to where the snow is off of Nursery. He said, "I don't know how we're going to get her in our car." I said, "Well, I'll put the top down on my convertible and we can put her in the back seat." They lifted her and set her down there and took sandbags and braced her leg. We took her down to the hospital. Then they reset her leg in the hospital. At that time, we had enough volunteers to help carry her down the deep snow until we got to where the car was.[85]

Stories of Safety and Rescue

Ski patrolling in the 1930s was quite informal, with those who had some first aid training taking the lead. Buck based the first aid training on what he had learned in the Boy Scouts, as well as later classes. The need for a more organized medical

Ski patrol first aid training at Casper College *(Photograph by Gay Nations)*

presence became more serious when Hogadon opened. Oda Sulley and Brendan Phibbs helped with first aid classes, as did Lou Demorest and Buck Weaver. After a time, they began holding classes at Casper College. Tim Weaver, who was a firefighter and paramedic, taught many classes over the years.

As the number of ski enthusiasts grew, so too did injuries. Glenn Bochmann told interviewers that at one point, a man hurt himself on Miner. Rob Robertson assessed him, and not having access to a toboggan, he put him over his shoulder and carried him to the top of the run. With a sled, they would have taken him to the bottom of the hill and then down to Dixie Lodge. Although the man had seemed to be seriously hurt, that was not, in fact, true. When Robertson put him down, he put his skis back on and skied away.[86]

Sometimes, beginners, pushing their skills beyond their limits, would be injured. And as organizers built more challenging runs, there were more opportunities for things to go wrong. In January 1949, ski patrollers made a point of warning beginners to stick to Nursery and stay off of runs such as Miner, Spillway, and Bumps-A-Daisy, but especially Thunderbolt, as there had been a number of injuries on that run in the weeks before the warning.[87]

In the early days, there was not too much training or equipment for rescues. For a long time, they were still using the old military surplus toboggan with the open front end.[88] People helping accident victims on Miner or Spillway could either pull them up to the road or carefully move them down the steep slope to Garden Creek and then down to Dixie Lodge. They used ropes and a bar on the front to steer the sled, descending slowly to keep the patient as safe as possible.[89]

Bob Kidd described how hard it was to get people off the slopes using the toboggans.

> Kidd: If somebody got hurt on Miner, you just had to pull them out of there physically because there was no place to go down below. That was [a] long ways from the highway.
>
> Weaver: You'd have to go down the draw, down to Dixie Lodge.
>
> Kidd: To go down Garden Creek. But those guys were big, tough. I don't remember ever seeing anybody evacuated from Miner. I do from the ski jump. But that was kind of over to the parking lot.[90]

Pinky Ellis remembered another accident on Miner.

> Pinky: A guy named Joe Robb came down. He didn't get stopped in time, and he ran his boots right underneath of the logs [at the bottom of Miner]. Broke both legs. I've never forgotten that. And there was no such thing as a ski patrol. Don't even remember that there was even an army rescue sled. I don't remember how we got him out of there, but it was a lot of tough pulling and yanking. If I remember right, we came out at Asbestos Spring. Is that possible? I think it is.
>
> Sam Weaver: You would have had to take him back up the hill to do that. Probably went down the canyon towards Dixie.[91]

Ski lifts contributed to their share of accidents, as did the disregard for basic safety rules. Doug French noted that at one point, his wife, Betty Jo, got her coat caught on the Hogadon T-bar and the operator had to stop the lift to get her down. She was not injured but was frightened by her experience.[92]

The layout of the slopes could cause injuries. Many who gave oral histories mentioned accidents in the early days of Hogadon. Bob Kidd remembered the day Ken Barnes wiped out on Boomerang. "But lots of horrific injuries. I had a coach, Ken Barnes. There used to be an island of trees right off the top of Boomerang in what now looks like a bowl. He said, 'Follow me.' Skied right into it. Stuck his leg out and had a compound fracture of the femur."[93]

Bruce Ladd described the time, when he was fourteen, that he broke his leg.

> I was skiing February 14, 1971. I was skiing over on the face. Bob Horstman, who was our ski doctor, was our across-the-street neighbor. I happened to climb up onto the Park Avenue face with him. We got to the top. We had the opportunity make fresh tracks. It was about one fifteen in the afternoon.
>
> He skied down ahead and stopped. And I skied up to him. We commented about how nice the snow was. Then I skied the rest of the way down. I got to the flats right there at Park Avenue. There was a creek there. It's kind of all leveled out now, but there was a creek there. And I happened to ski with one foot over a fallen tree and one foot under. I remember my shin hitting that tree and pitching forward. And I heard my leg break. Bob skied up and says, "How are you doing?" I said, "Well, I broke my leg." And he says, "How do you know?" And I said, "Because I heard it." And he says, "Well, that's a definite something."
>
> So, he contacted the ski patrol. And I rode up in the sled. He had a brand-new BMW, 2002 coupe. I had always wanted to ride in that car. Well, this was my first chance. He drove me down the mountain. We went right to the hospital. He X-rayed. Said, "Yeah, it's a spiral fracture. It hasn't slipped. I don't have to do any adjustments, just a straight cast." He put a cast on and drove me home.
>
> My parents were at a Girl Scouts event with my sister, Lee Anne. They came home and found me sitting there with my ski pants cut off—at least the one leg, the right leg—and then a cast on. They said, "How'd that happen?" "Well, I was skiing with Dr. Horstman."[94]

There were a number of rules that were designed to keep the slopes safer for everyone. When skiers, usually young ones, broke too many rules, there was a box that they called a penalty box in the patrol hut. Scofflaws' names and the infraction went into the box, and after too many penalties, management kicked them off the mountain and denied them the right to come back. They could also mark a skier's lift ticket with a red mark which became an X with multiple infractions. That got that skier kicked off the slopes for the rest of that day.[95] That usually saved a few people from accidents due to sheer stupidity.

When snowboarders first started coming to Hogadon, there were safety problems. This was partly due to them not knowing the rules, and many boarders tended to be a bit wild. The boarders also used the slopes differently than skiers. This caused an extended and uncomfortable breaking in period for both groups.

Bill Ladd noted some of the issues in his interview.

> Another thing: skiers are a little more educated in knowing what a boarder is going to do. With a skier, you can watch and get an idea that they're going to turn one way or the other. With the boarder, you had no idea. So, I never get on the blind side of a boarder if I can help it. Because you don't know what he's going to do, and he can't see me. So, I'm more educated and I can stay away. And I think the boarders are growing into an older group. You have rowdy kids on skis, and you have rowdy kids on boards.[96]

The other issue was that boarders had different types of injuries, which required some changes in first aid training.[97] Jan and Bill Chambers shared a story from 2019 that reflected the challenges of dealing with snowboarding injuries.

> Bill: We had that femur four weeks ago. A boarder.
> Jan: Hit the tower.
> Bill: The kid had been pushing his luck all season. He'd been skiing down the lift line.

Jan: Fast.
Bill: And hit the pad. Broke the femur. They had a hard time getting him out because he'd sunk down into the tower well a little bit. So, they had to use a scoop splint. It took a while to get him out. Ambulance came up and Life Flight came up. We had to shut off— we don't have an actual landing zone for helicopters, so we had to shut off the parking lot so the guy could land. So, Life Flight's up there, the ambulance is up there. And the worst part of the whole thing was the roads were terrible coming up.
Jan: That was the night they shut them down, in fact. And the wind was very gusty and so the helicopter was just, it was a little bit scary watching it. But, boy, he set it down.
MaryAnn: So, they just landed in the parking lot now?
Bill: Yeah, we just shut off. Somebody shuts the road off where it splits off to Micro Road. Then we block traffic. We don't have a wind sock any more. So, we're standing there with a little fluorescent thing to try and let him know where the wind gusts are.
Jan: It was so gusty, everybody holding things, one pointing one way, the other one pointing the other way. He went down in the ambulance. Then shortly after, they shut the road.
Bill: So, it would have been interesting because we would have had an injured person in an ambulance stuck on the road. And the conditions too bad for the helicopter to come in, and there wouldn't have been an LZ [landing zone] for him anyway. But the last we heard, he was in surgery, so I don't know what. Anyway, that's the last.[98]

Bill Chambers, talking about rescues, highlighted a piece of equipment they used to extract injured skiers.

For a while, we had "Herv." I don't know if we talked about "Herv." "Herv" was a tracked vehicle that would meet us at the bottom, a snowcat. Then you would load them in, and "Herv" would go up to the top and we'd unload them and put them in the hut and do whatever you needed to. But "Herv" was so rough. It was terrible. Clank, clank, clank. They tried everything to get it comfortable. We tried inner tubes that we put the boat on. I mean, it was awful. Somebody would have to ride up with them to make sure that they were all right. Which is another thing that we always have to do. Because when you're transporting them up, you always have to know what's going on with them. If they start to get sick, you got a problem. You've got to get something to clear their airway. So "Herv" was kind of a stopgap. We don't do that anymore.[99]

Training Patrollers

MaryAnn Hoff was actively involved in the ski patrol for decades. She described the training over the years.

When I first got on the patrol, which was in 1969–1970, we had American Red Cross first aid. Period. A small little book. And it was actually first aid. I remember [Dr.] Oda Sulley was one of our instructors. We had to get our credentials for American Red Cross first aid at that time. It was very *first aid.* Then it started getting a little bit more complicated and a little bit more complicated. And now the manual that they have is *Outdoor Emergency Care.* And it's a book. Every time they revise it—and I think they're revising it again—so, they add more stuff. So, you really have to know a lot about emergency care now.

You go to training every year. We have an outdoor emergency care [training]. It's a half day or a day. Well, it's a day long now. But you go through the practical portions. And you have to perform—they have simulated things that you have to take care of as you go.

Then the CPR [cardiopulmonary resuscitation] got more complicated. Now, it's basic life support. But now we have the AED [automatic external defibrillator]. So, the AED, when they first came out, they were saying, "We can get the AED when the emergency people come up." But now the AED is readily available; it's right there in the patrol hut. We all know how to use it, to shock someone if they have a need for it. So, it's just become quite complicated now. Quite hard.

To be on the ski patrol, you have to pass a test. You have to be able to handle a toboggan. You have a written test. Then one of the things you had to do, you had to walk from the bottom of the hill to the top of the hill, and then ski back down. They'd take you into the crud to make sure you could ski the crud. It wasn't very pretty sometimes.[100]

Lou Demorest had been a mountain safety trainer up in Montana. He brought that to Casper Mountain, working with Jerry Schiller, Howie Bronsdon, and others. He took those interested in mountain safety to Togwotee Pass near the Tetons for mountain-rescue training.

Bill Chambers remembered one trip.

Bill: And we dug snow caves and snow pits and all that. Spent the night. Then coming down, we had our cooking gear. Coming down—we had converted downhill skis with Silvetta bindings, basic stuff. Poor Gay Nations. With pots and pans strapped to him. We got pans and pots and Gay tumbling down this hill.

Jan: Literal ass over teakettle.[101]

Eventually, they were not just responsible for Hogadon but also for much of the mountain, including finding lost snowmobilers and monitoring the cross-country trails.[102] Demorest and his team also taught junior patrollers-in-training winter survival by teaching them how to build snow caves for shelter.

Top: **Howie Bronsdon digs a snow cave during a mountain-survival training day.** *(Photograph by Gay Nations)* Bottom: **New patrollers** *(Photograph by Gay Nations)*

Top: **Tim Weaver and a friend stand at the entrance of their emergency snow cave shelter.** *(Photograph by Gay Nations)* Bottom: **Tim Weaver at the Hawaiian-themed ski patrol party** *(Photograph by Gay Nations)*

After a class graduated, there was a party, which the new patrollers put together. They brought up food and beer and often had themes. Jan Chambers remembered that one year, it was a Hawaiian theme. They would gather at someone's house. Some people had memories of parties at Buck Weaver's cabin. But mostly, they held them in the lodge or the patrol hut. Sometimes, they would invite Bob Hardesty, who was the manager at that time. And sometimes, the "lifties" who ran the tows came as well. The parties involved music and dancing. Stan DeVore played his banjo.[103]

How the Patrol Did Its Work
MaryAnn Hoff shared her experiences in the ski patrol.

Well, I became a regular patroller. And I found a little cheat sheet because I couldn't have remembered it. I was in auxiliary, starting in '70. And I became a regular patroller in '72. Which means I got to wear the jacket. Then I got another level, [for] which I got a cool little pin, the national pin. And I became a national in 1985. Which is kind of an honor. You have to meet certain criteria and then you get your national appointment.[104]

But there were so many people that came through the patrol. Every year, we'd have three or four or five and sometimes ten new ones. We usually had a roster of like a total of fifty people on the ski patrol at any one time. That was divided into four crews. We had A, B, C, and D crews. I was always on B crew. You'd have a day leader. The day leaders— well, before the city started buying stuff, we had to buy all of our own equipment and radios. And we had our own toboggans. So, we'd have fundraisers. We had to do that. And then the city came in and started helping somewhat.

So, you'd have the four crews. We tried to have at least seven people on a crew on the weekend. These were weekend crews. You could ski during the week any time. They were always happy to have you come up to help get coverage on the hill. But then you'd have standbys. So, if you couldn't make your crew day, then you were responsible to get somebody to go up.

Sometimes, we'd have three people in the patrol hut that had been injured. When an accident came in, there was always somebody in the patrol hut. You had your times during the day that you sat in the patrol hut. Sometimes, you had a time that you'd sit at the top of Bunny [Hill].

So, the accident report would come in. Right away, you'd have somebody else in there that would be ready to go to the accident. They'd go check it out. Call up for their equipment. Start the first aid on the hill. Then call for however many people they needed on the accident. They'd ski them down in the toboggan to the lift.

At first, we didn't have a snowcat or anything to take them up in. Take them up behind the T-bar.

And then it got to a little bit more complicated when we got the chair. They'd be loaded into the snowcat, the toboggan and take it up on Bunny Hill. If there was something that needed a helicopter, or something real serious, the person who was on the accident first would call in, and then they'd have contact with the hospital. That was how that happened.[105]

Pat Harshman added additional details on the ski patrol's rescue routine.

Then you stay out and you just systematically go from different runs, just constantly checking everything. If there's a report of an injury, then we lately are trying to stay in flow with all of the other EMS [emergency medical services] services with the ICS [incident command system], which is a way of directing a scene so to speak. So, you have your person in command who gives assignments to the other patrollers.[106]

We have one patroller that's in the patrol hut. But we see if there's anybody else a little bit closer that can respond faster than from the patrol hut. They go out, they do a patient assessment. Decide what is needed as far as splints, first aid needing to be rendered, and transportation. So, depending on what it is, the patroller in the patrol hut, if he didn't go out immediately on the call, then he starts taking equipment down and assists the first patroller on scene. Then everything is coordinated through the patrol hut so that we know what equipment to send and if we need to call the ambulance and other things.

We used to be able to call the hospital emergency room directly and talk to either a paramedic, a nurse, or a doctor and request an ambulance. We always put it on them as to what they will send, especially when Life Flight came into being.

It was in [pause] like '83, somewhere in there. I know they were looking at Life Flight back then.

I don't think we used it a whole lot up at Hogadon initially. Then for a while, they sent it on everything. It became quite painful, and we had customers calling and saying, "My child didn't need that. Why did you do it?" Then it was nice that we could say, "Well, we just inform the hospital what we have, and they choose to send what they send."[107]

And on daily routine:

I don't think when I initially got on patrol that there was quite— I mean, we did mark hazards with the bamboo, but not as much as what we do now. The opening and the closing of the area to where we're doing what we call sweeps, where we're out there and we have to beat the customers out and try to get as much done as we can. Of course, we can't get every single run before opening, so we're trying to get the runs. We are risk managers of the area. So, we need to check if there's any ruts that somebody could get caught up in, left from the groomer. If there's any rocks that rolled from any of the rocky areas out onto the slope that would send someone flying or a sudden stop and send them flying.

There's been various things throughout the years that have had to be marked or mitigated to keep people safe. Our area, we used to be able to go out of bounds. But the private landowners around Hogadon have requested that the skiers don't. So, we don't go off area. But we still have places on the area that can avalanche and slide. So, we have to watch those situations. Nobody's been buried very deep, more than up to their waist or their chest. But it still happens.

On one of our newer runs, when we first opened it, it has slid on patrollers and we've had to close it back down for it to get firmed up.

We've gone from just having to sign in just to keep track of how many patrols they used to put in per season, to all sorts of paperwork that is required by our insurance and downtown risk manager. From marking down the sweeps and noting hazards that you've mitigated to the hour marked. Opening and closing runs have to be kept track of.

So, you have your daily paperwork. Which goes on all day long. So, from signing up clear through signing out, we have three official sweeps of the day where you're looking at surface conditions in addition to any hazards. You take care of hazards when you come across them.

Then the medical form has grown vastly. And you really have to document a whole bunch of things now on the medical forms when we're treating somebody.[108]

The ski patrol spends a lot of time and money training so that they are prepared to take care of any medical emergency. They train at yearly division meetings and then hold yearly refreshers for Casper patrollers. Courses include outdoor emergency care, CPR, chair evacuation, and toboggan safety.

Behind the Scenes

There was a lot of work off the slopes as well. For many years, ski patrol members bought their own gear and even many of the first aid supplies. Although the city eventually began to budget for basic first aid and rescue items, the ski patrol has always held fundraising events to purchase safety equipment, radios, medical supplies, materials for training meetings, and awards. They even helped—with money and labor—in the construction of patrol huts.[109]

Both Marilyn Ladd and Jan Chambers patrolled, but they also served on the board, helped with fundraisers, and even provided snacks for patrollers to have after a long day. Jan, who had joined in the 1964–65 season, was on patrol for fifty-three years. She noted that there were many other women who had been there in the beginning, including Joyce Garberg and Joanne Taylor.

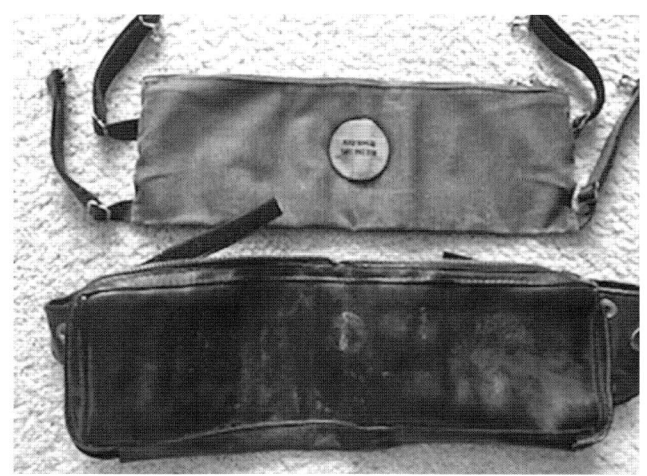

Top: **Patrollers wore these packs to carry basic first aid materials. Each person owned their own.** *(Hoff collection)* Bottom: **Ski patrol Head skis raffle poster** *(Weaver-Hunt collection)*

Jan provided some good insights as to what went on behind the scenes. Jan became second assistant patrol leader for two years, then first assistant for another two years, and then patrol leader for two years. As second assistant, she got equipment ready and provided supplies for the patrol hut. It was mostly being the go-to for first aid. She also helped with getting the Warren Miller movies set up. The movie showing each year was a big fundraiser for the ski patrol. During her time, they showed the film at the NCHS, at the American Theatre, and eventually at the Event Center. They showed the movie for several nights. It was a huge undertaking with booths for vendors, and it required the involvement of the entire patrol. Each patroller sold tickets. The biggest sellers were Bob Hardesty and Donald Wolcott. They sold hundreds of tickets each. The movie really started off the ski season.

Another fundraiser was the raffling off of new skis. MaryAnn made a list of other innovative fundraisers. They included the following: "When Hardesty was area manager, he paid patrollers $10 a day to be at top of Bunny Hill to 'untangle skiers' at the top of the rope tow. Sold Christmas trees. Raffles such as the Booze or Beef Basket. Working concessions at Event Center selling hot dogs, popcorn, beer, etc., for 20 percent of sales. Black Diamond Dinner with wine tasting."[110]

As patrol leader, Jan also ran the annual ski patrol business meeting. At that time, they had about seventy members. For a time, they also had a speaker who talked about something of interest to skiers.[111]

End of a Ski Day

At the end of the day, the ski patrollers had additional duties. They would make a last sweep that hopefully caught anyone who had taken one last run after closing hours or who was out of bounds or on a remote trail and was injured. Bill Chambers described this end-of-day routine in the oral history conducted by MaryAnn Hoff and Sandy Leotta.

Bill: Then, as far as what we did back then, we did our duties, we ran our sweeps at the end of the day, made sure nobody was left on a hill. Then we could not take our boots off or leave until everybody was accounted for in the parking lot. If they weren't accounted for, then we were responsible for going out. We had a set search and rescue plan, where we would check the various runs, inside the lodge.

Jan: Especially if there were cars left in the parking lot.

Sandy: If people had been skiing through the trees or whatever, you didn't have to check through the trees, did you?

Bill: We hollered a lot. And we would hope that they would respond. But if somebody's not around— We still do that, except that I don't think we've had anybody left. Then with the lodge open now, people are staying later.

Jan: We now have radios and cell phones, which makes a huge difference from what we used to have. We would follow tracks through trees if we thought somebody might still be around there. Had gone off area a little bit. You followed his tracks in a little bit and holler.

MaryAnn: Instead of just skiing down the hill, you'd stop every little ways—not just at the bottom of the hill—and holler that the area was closed. So that anybody would be warned that if they were still out and about.

Bill: That was the T-bar era. With some of the things that would happen, people would try and poach one last run. They would fall off the T-bar halfway up Dreadnaught.[112]

Equipment and Facilities

The buildings changed over the years. At first it was the A-frame. Jerry Schilling described it in his interview for the ski history project.

MaryAnn: But what about the years in the A-frame? Because the A-frame was there when you started. Talk about that one.

Jerry: That was pretty primitive. Even the warming hut was kind of non-existent at the time. So, that was just about the time I started, though, so I didn't really spend too much time in that.

MaryAnn: How was that little A-frame heated?

Jerry: It was a wood stove.

MaryAnn: At the end, and then benches along the side, as I remember.

Jerry: Yeah, benches along the side. No examination tables, really no niceties. At the time, again, the philosophy was immediate and temporary. So, the idea was to get them off the hill, package and ship them down.

Sandy: And that hut didn't have room for more than about four to five people, is that correct? That A-frame?

Jerry: Oh, actually, there was quite a bit of room. I don't know. I guess it would be probably maybe twenty feet long. There wasn't any excess room, for sure. But I don't remember any examination tables or anything like that in there. And

Exterior of the original ski patrol hut *(Photograph by Gay Nations)*

we'd bring a toboggan in and get somebody splinted up. All of the splints at that time were kind of homemade. Wooden and lined with foam rubber. You'd lace them up. Again, very primitive. You'd package and haul.[113]

In 2014, a new, badly needed ski patrol hut and maintenance building were budgeted for by the city. It was dropped from the budget, and a plan was put in place to redefine the scope of the project due to the deteriorating lodge and lifts and the inadequate space for the ski patrol, the ski school, racers, and the rental shop. That was the beginning of the plan and realization of the beautiful new facilities at Hogadon, which opened the summer of 2017. Many of the patrollers—as well as other ski groups, "Friends of Hogadon," and community leaders—made this dream a reality.[114]

Some Final Words on the Ski Patrol

The following final words come from MaryAnn Hoff.

Top: **Interior of the old patrol hut; Sam Weaver and Gay Nations** *(Gay Nations collection)* Bottom: **Patrollers Sean Ellis, Jerry Schilling, and Jan Chambers waiting for a rescue call in the second patrol building.** *(Photograph by Gay Nations)*

The Casper Mountain Ski Patrol started as a loosely organized group of skiers who knew a little basic first aid and had a lot of dedication to supporting skiing and development of the early ski runs on Casper Mountain. The ski pioneers took care of injured skiers as best they could. The Ski Patrol continued to learn and evolved into a professional, emergency medical service to the outdoor recreation community on Casper Mountain. When Hogadon Ski Area opened in 1959, the Casper Mountain Ski Patrol, CMSP, volunteers assumed the role of keeping skiers safe and rescuing injured skiers at Hogadon as well as Nordic skiers and other Casper Mountain outdoor enthusiasts. Most members of the Patrol are volunteers with a few paid Pro Patrollers. At present 2021 – Ryan Butler

Top: **Casper Mountain Ski Patrol group photo, 1995** *(Gay Nations collection)* Right: These are the names of all of the ski patrol members in 1995. *(Photograph by Gay Nations)*

Bottom Row - Left to Right
Shawn Mammon, Mike Keim, Pinky Ellis, Jim Barton, Mark McAtee, Sandy Nations, Dan Rea, (?transferred back to Michigan), Ken Hoff, Doug Follick, Gary VanTrease, Don Wolcott, Pete Bue, Jerod Levine, Kathy Doing, Kent Doing

Middle Row - Left to Right
Sean Ellis, Jerry Schilling, Robert Walker, Mike McLemore, Andy Dahill, Dave Nichols (Patrol Leader), Steve Lovelace, Chris Muth, Ken Chastek, Debbie Huber, Lisa Wolcott, Pat Harshman, Mary Ann Hoff, Bill Bays, Willie Walkinshaw, Rush Bartlett, Jeff Wilcox, Liz Ohlrogge, Dick Brehm, Karen Zimmerman, Heidi Palmer, George Brown, Ralph Barton, Bruce English

Top Row - Left to Right
Brendan Ellis, Kim Weikum, Tom Weckwerth, Ken Ohlrogge, Bill Maiers, Darrell Carruth (2nd Assistant PL), Helen Schilling, Eric Easton (1st Assistant PL), Everett Akam, Robert McComas, Dave Davis, Steve Cathey, Pete Steinbrenner, Gay Nations, Sam Weaver, Chris Icenogle, Tim Weaver, Jan Chambers, Jim Colva, Brad Ward, Bill Chambers

Picture taken October 1995, Pineview School Yard - First Aid Refresher

and Joel Simonson are the only paid patrollers since Pat Harshman recently retired. Mark Bower is the NSPS Casper Mountain Ski Patrol Director.[115]

Casper mountain's group built a reputation for professionalism, preparation, and safety.[116] The volunteer organization is good about recognizing leadership. They give a number of awards. The following is a Casper Mountain Ski Patrol partial list of awards: Outstanding Junior Patroller in the Nation – Sean Ellis, 1973; Outstanding Ski Patrolman in the Nation – Fred Klein, 1971; Outstanding Patroller in the Northern Division – Bill Chambers, 1983; Gay Nations, 1986; MaryAnn Hoff, 2005–2006.[117]

In the 1970–71 season, they won an NSP outstanding patroller in the nation award. They also got the "Friends of Minnie Dole trophy." (CMSP was the smallest out of one thousand patrols in nation.) In 1972, they hosted the National Ski Patrol meeting at Hogadon. The festivities included a party at Jerry Shilling's home and a rodeo at his neighbor's ranch.[118]

Although they have added professional, paid patrollers, they still have a solid and stalwart core of dedicated members. In the spring of 2021, the ski patrol director is Mark Bower.[119]

Left: When the National Ski Patrol met in Casper, the attendees were treated to a rodeo. *(Photograph by Gay Nations)* Right: Gay Nations at the rodeo *(Gay Nations collection)*

NOTES

1. Bill Bon, Casper Mountain Ski History Project, oral history interview by Sam Weaver, November 10, 2013, 6.

2. US Ski and Snowboard Hall of Fame, accessed June 24, 2020, https://skihall.com/hall-of-famers/thor-c-groswold/.

3. Fred Walters, Casper Mountain Ski History Project, oral history interview by Sam Weaver, October 31, 2015, 1.

4. Walters, interview, 2–3.

5. Barry Horn, Casper Mountain Ski History Project, oral history interview by Sam Weaver, April 27, 2013, 6.

6. Angus Morrison, Casper Mountain Ski History Project, oral history interview by Sam Weaver, April 7, 2009, 5.

7. Bob Kidd, e-mail, August 24, 2019.

8. Morrison, interview, 6.

9. Bob Kidd, e-mail, August 18, 2019.

10. Bon, interview, 2.

11. Morrison, interview, 4–5.

12. Morrison, interview, 7.

13. Morrison, interview, 6.

14. Bob Kidd in Bruce Lamberson, Casper Mountain Ski History Project, oral history interview by MaryAnn Hoff and Sandy Leotta, n.d., 13.

15. Glenn Bochmann, Casper Mountain Ski History Project, oral history interview by Sam Weaver, April 25, 2011, 7.

16. Bill Garberg, Casper Mountain Ski History Project, oral history interview by Sam Weaver, August 22, 2016, 4.

17. Bob Hardesty, Casper Mountain Ski History Project, oral history interview by Sam Weaver and Sean Ellis, January 3, 2011, 7.

18. Garberg, interview, 4.

19. Morrison, interview, 6.

20. Chris Smith, Casper Mountain Ski History Project, oral history interview by MaryAnn Hoff and Sandy Leotta, February 17, 2019, 16–17.

21. Garberg, interview, 4.

22. Garberg, interview, 4.

23. Bruce Ladd, Casper Mountain Ski History Project, oral history interview by Sandy Leotta and MaryAnn Hoff, January 23, 2019, 7.

24. Bill and Marilyn Ladd, Casper Mountain Ski History Project, oral history interview by Sam Weaver interviewer, November 22, 2014, 13.

25. Garberg, interview, 12.

26. Garberg, interview, 5.

27. Garberg, intereview, 5–6.

28. Garberg, interview, 12.

29. Garberg and Sam Weaver in Garberg, interview, 12.

30. Diane Neste, e-mail to Sandy Leotta, 2021.

31. Christina Schmidt, "Vantrease: 'Time for me to move on,'" *Casper Journal*, May 2012.

32. Smith, interview, 8–9.

33. Morrison, interview, 6.

34. Horn, interview, 6/7.

35. Horn, interview, 6/7.

36. Sandy Leotta, Casper Mountain Ski History Project, oral history interview by MaryAnn Hoff, September 22, 2020, 5.

37. Horn, interview, 7.

38. "First Annual Hogadon Ski Races Scheduled for Sunday," *Casper Tribune-Herald*, February 18, 1960, 16.

39. Bochmann, interview, 11–12.

40. Leotta, 7.

41. Leotta, 7.

42. Bill and Marilyn Ladd, Casper Mountain Ski History Project, oral history interview by Sam Weaver, November 22, 2014, 9.

43. Chris Bochmann, "Slalom Sam," *Casper Tribune-Herald*, 1958.

44. Bochmann, "Slalom Sam," n.p.

45. "Ski Meet Saturday," *Casper Star-Tribune*, March 30, 1967, 18.

46. Bruce Ladd, interview, 5.

47. Bruce Lamberson, Casper Mountain Ski History Project, oral history interview by MaryAnn Hoff and Sandy Leotta, n.d., 13.

48. Tom Stroock, Casper Mountain Ski History Project, oral history interview by Sam Weaver and Sean Ellis, n.d., 5–6.

49. Jim Weiss obituary, Jones and Casey Funeral Home, Salmon, Idaho, January 25, 2021.

50. Weiss obituary.

51. Stroock, interview, 6.

52. Bruce Ladd, interview, 5.

53. Sandy Leotta, e-mail, January 22, 2021.

54. Bruce Ladd, interview, 9–10.

55. Walters, interview, 5, 7.

56. Bruce Ladd, interview, 5.

57. Leotta, interview, 2.

58. Leotta, interview,10

59. Cam Walker, Casper Mountain Ski History Project, oral history interview by Sandy Leotta and MaryAnn Hoff, March 21, 2019, 5–6.

60. Smith, interview, 19–20.

61. Bruce Ladd, interview, 4–5.

62. "New Tow Placed on Mountain Run," *Casper Tribune-Herald*, 1948.

63. *The Chinook*, Casper Junior College, November 16, 1951, 5.

64. Garberg, interview, 13.

65. Walker, interview, 19.

66. Bob Kidd, Casper Mountain Ski History Project, oral history interview by Sam Weaver, November 15, 2014, 8.

67. Sandy Leotta, e-mail to Rebecca Hunt, January 2021, 1.

68. Laurie Weaver, Casper Mountain Ski History Project, oral history interview by MaryAnn Hoff and Sandy Leotta, January 16, 2019, 15–16.

69. Weaver, interview, 5.

70. Weaver, interview, 15–16.

71. Weaver, interview, 16.

72. Smith, interview, 1–2.

73. Smith, interview, 6.

74. National Ski Patrol official website, accessed August 27, 2020, https://nspserves.org/history/.

75. US National Ski and Snowboard Hall of Fame, "Roger Langley: Hall of Fame Class of 1958," accessed August 27, 2020, https://skihall.com/hall-of-famers/roger-langley/.

76. Cathleen Norman, *Loveland Ski Area: Colorado's Best-Known Secret* (Virginia Beach, VA: The Donning Publishing Company, 2014), 130.

77. "Patrol Protects Skiers," *Casper Star-Tribune*, January 17, 1964.

78. "Patrol Protects Skiers."

79. MaryAnn Hoff, note to Rebecca Hunt, May 2021, 1.

80. MaryAnn Hoff, notes to Rebecca Hunt, May 2021.

81. "The Masked Cavaliers," *Casper Magazine* 3, no. 14 (February/March 1980), 10.

82. Morrison, interview, 10.

83. Charlie Peak, Casper Mountain Ski History Project, oral history interview by Sam Weaver, October 30, 2016, 4.

84. Morrison, interview, 9.

85. Morrison, interview, 9.

86. Bochmann, interview, 5.

87. *Casper Herald-Tribune*, January 9, 1949, n.p.

88. Morrison, interview, 9–10.

89. Horn, interview, 8.

90. Kidd, interview, 13.

91. Frank (Pinky) Ellis, Casper Mountain Ski History Project, oral history interview by Sam Weaver, January 3, 2014, 4.

92. Doug French, Casper Mountain Ski History Project, oral history interview by Sam Weaver and Sean Ellis, August 8, 2009, 6.

93. Kidd, interview, 13.

94. Bruce Ladd, interview, 2.

95. Bill and Janet Chambers, Casper Mountain Ski History Project, oral history interview by MaryAnn Hoff and Sandy Leotta, April 4, 2019, 6.

96. Bill Chambers in Bill and Janet Chambers, interview, 7.

97. Bill Chambers in Bill and Janet Chambers, interview, 11.

98. Bill Chambers in Bill and Janet Chambers, interview, 12–13.

99. Bill Chambers in Bill and Janet Chambers, interview, 13.

100. MaryAnn Hoff, Casper Mountain Ski History Project, oral history interview by Sandy Leotta, September 22, 2020, 5–7.

101. Janet Chambers in Bill and Janet Chambers, interview, 19.

102. Jerry Schilling, Casper Mountain Ski History Project, oral history interview by Sandy Leotta and MaryAnn Hoff, January 2021, 10–11.

103. Janet Chambers in Bill and Janet Chambers, interview, 27.

104. Hoff, interview, 3.

105. Hoff, interview, 6–7.

106. Pat Harshman, Casper Mountain Ski History Project, oral history interview by MaryAnn Hoff and Sandy Leotta, February 5, 2019, 11–12.

107. Harshman, interview, 10.

108. Harshman, interview, 9–10.

109. MaryAnn Hoff, e-mail, 1.

110. Hoff, e-mail, 1–2.

111. Janet Chambers in Bill and Janet Chambers, interview, 2–3.

112. Bill and Janet Chambers, interview, 11–12.

113. Schilling, interview, 5–6.

114. Hoff, e-mail, 2.

115. Hoff, e-mail, 1.

116. Bob Kidd, e-mail to Rebecca Hunt, February 15, 2021.

117. Hoff, e-mail, 2.

118. Schilling, interview, 4.

119. *Polaris*, Official Publication of the Northern Division of the National Ski Patrol (Spring 2021), 27.

CHAPTER FIVE

Casper Mountain Cross-Country

The Casper Nordic Ski Team runs on the East End Road on Casper Mountain. (*Casper Nordic Ski Team collection*)

*B*ACK WHEN SKIING WAS A FORM OF TRANSPORTATION, cross-country was the original way to get around in the winter. Nils Fougstedt, after arriving in Wyoming in the 1920s, not only encouraged an interest in downhill (Alpine) skiing but also in cross-country (Nordic). He was the founder of the Thunderbolt ski run, cutting the original run in the 1920s. Nils often visited neighbors using either skis or snowshoes. A description of Nils's mountain life said that "he played bridge all evening and then skied cross-country all day."[1]

Neal Forsling described Nils and his visits with neighbors, this time on snowshoes. "Nils was not a tall man but there was nothing frail about him. He was compact and strongly muscled from lifting an ax and letting it fall with a stroke into the heart of a tree. His eyes were the Swedish blue and his whiskers were red. He usually wore a Stetson pushed back on his head. He loved to bake fresh bread, many loaves at a time, then he would start out on his snowshoes with a loaf or two in his knapsack."[2]

Another mountain resident was Dave Crockett, a miner who had many claims across the mountain top. Neal also commented on his travels in winter. "Dave took most things seriously. He was dead in earnest about mining and was living on the mountain all the year around. He had plenty of time to brood over his mining claims and would go about on skis to see that no one had jumped them."[3]

Nils's brother, Ole Fougstedt, frequently described his own ski journeys around the snowy mountain as he built cabins, checked on friends, or tended the tow motor at the Nursery hill. He also documented the comings and goings of friends who skied in to visit him. Neal Forsling often mentioned her husband's (Jim's) trips in and out in the winter.[4] When Jack and Jewell Cummings moved to the

Up the mountain, March 27, 1926. Gladys and Cy Bon are on the right. *(Bill Bon collection)*

mountain, they too used skis and snowshoes to get from place to place.[5]

Even after a variety of downhill slopes opened, many of the more expert skiers would end a day (for instance, on Nursery) by taking a late-day or moonlight run across large swaths of Casper Mountain. The oral history interviews with pioneer skiers documented these cross-country adventures. One popular destination was Eadsville, the abandoned mining town on the western end of the mountain. And some mountain residents simply skied across the mountain to get to a day of downhill.[6]

In 1936, the Casper Mountain Ski Club, working with Casper mayor Frank Cowan, began to market cross-country skiing as a wholesome family outing. Sometimes, as many as sixty or seventy people would gather at Nursery, ski down its back side, go to the Lions' Club camp, and then come back.

Top: Jewell Cummings uses snowshoes to get around outside of her home, Wa-Wa Lodge. *(Julie York collection)* Bottom: This map details the extent of the Natrona County Nordic Trails system on Casper Mountain. *(Natrona County Parks collection)*

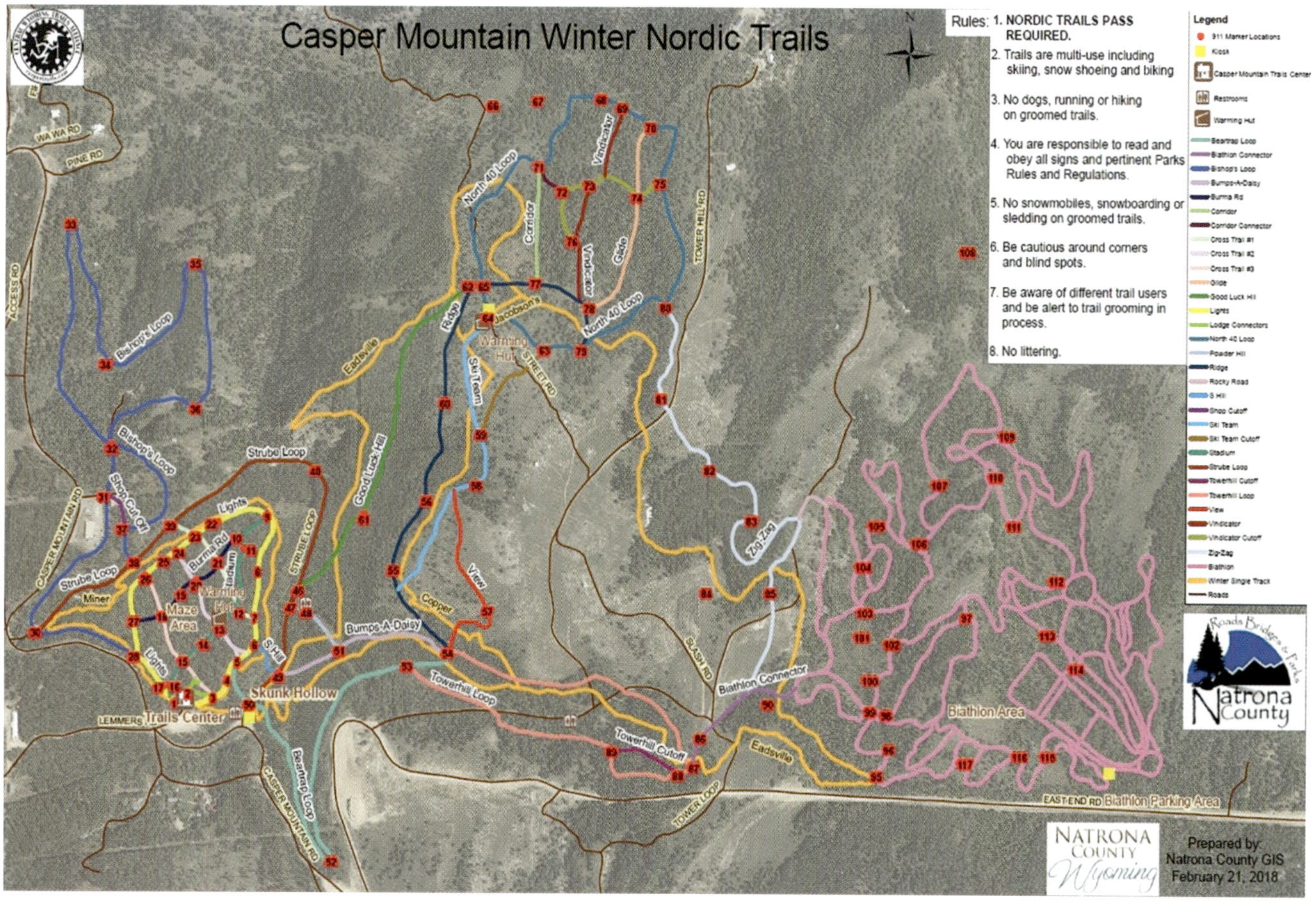

Casper Mountain Winter Nordic Trails

Angie Morrison remembered that at one time, there was a tow on the backside of Nursery to accommodate returning cross-country enthusiasts.[7]

Around this same time, the Civilian Conservation Corps (CCC) not only helped set up the first ski jump at Bumps-a-Daisy but also helped lay out both a slalom run and cross-country trails in the same area. These trails ran across the midline of the hill in a gentle grade from Beartrap Park to the trailhead at Skunk Hollow. With assistance from the ski club, the young CCC workers put in a tow as well.

Between 1935 and the beginning of World War II, there were Nordic, Alpine, and jumping competitions each year. Although ski numbers declined during the war, the interest in cross-country skiing remained. Military personnel on leave from the Casper Army Air Base spent as much time as possible on the mountain, discovering the slopes and trails and then revisiting their favorite haunts across the mountain.

Early equipment had to work for both downhill and cross-country.[8] Skis were long and made of wood. There was not much access to newer gear. But a few people were starting ski stores, mostly focused on downhill skiing. One that catered to cross-country skiers was owned by Miles Hecker, who also sold bicycles.[9] Hecker was a bicyclist, skier, mountaineer, and photographer.[10]

In a short document written in 2013, Dorothy Bullard recalled how she and her husband, Mike, helped popularize cross-country skiing on Casper Mountain.

> It is exciting to ski the Maze on perfectly groomed trails with young racers in training, families on a mountain outing, the eager physical fitness and peaceful meditation buffs as well as many of the old guard who have stayed with the sport for many years. It wasn't always like this. Now it is a nice cozy warm up lodge with food and hot drinks, high school racers dedicated to a sport which offers little glamour or recognition, Sunday lessons for dozens of kids interested in the sport.

> We (the Bullards) weren't the first cross country skiers in or around Casper. I remember a story of an older neighbor from Jackson Street. His name was Porter Davis, a vet of WWII, who skied with friends across the west end of the mountain to Goose Egg. Their wives were waiting and although they were very late getting there, to the concern of the wives, they finally arrived and had a nice dinner at the inn. Later, there were others, like Don Jacobson and Ken Hoff. While we were not the first, we did seem to help popularize the sport and create a social aspect which spread interest to others.[11]

Dorothy also noted the following.

> In 1972, Mike and Dorothy Bullard, newlyweds who visited Driggs, Idaho on their honeymoon, had "discovered" the sport of cross-country skiing. Dorothy was a downhill skier having learned while in college at the University of Wyoming and Mike was an import from Texas working in the oil field who had never been on skis. Wanting a mutual pastime that would take them into the mountains in winter, the couple pursued a gentler skiing experience even though there was no place in Casper to purchase equipment. The couple had gotten hold of a catalogue from REI and eagerly ordered equipment to begin their outdoor adventure. Soon several other couples became interested asking Mike to order equipment for them and our garage, on Fremont Street in the Fort Casper addition of Casper, became a pseudo ski shop smelling of pine tar and wax.

> In addition to Mike and Dorothy there were several couples who formed this early day cross country ski club: Kathy and Frank Fox, Bucky and Jennifer Walker, Dick and Robin Stein, Marty and Tom Stroh, Jan and Gib Tafoya. In the winter of 1972, we met weekly with our bota bags full of wine, some cheese

and sausages to cook over an open fire. We skied from the K2 tower toward the Girl Scout camp or the "bowl" or down Lions' Camp Road to Bear Trap Meadow and back. We skied out the old two track east end road across Crimson Dawn Park where we would stop for a picnic. We skied to Powder House shelter and all points in and around Beartrap Meadow. We all wore knickers in those days with colorful snowflake knee high stockings. We had to wear gaiters as we tracked all our own trails through often deep snow. There were fewer fences and no trespassing signs in those days, a friendlier atmosphere. We could go pretty much anywhere on the mountain and it was fun to create a new adventure each time we skied.[12]

After Mike and Dorothy Bullard decided to do more than sell gear out of their garage, they set up a shop in 1972 in the Laverty Building on West Second Street, next door to Goedicke's Art Supplies.[13] They called their store Cross Country Mountaineering, often shortened to CCM. The store also sold camping and mountaineering equipment. When Mike Bullard decided to take an oil job in Nigeria, they took on

This is the sort of informal trail created and used by early cross-country skiers. (*Photograph by Cathy Holman*)

partners Gib and Jan Tafoya to run the shop. The Bullards functioned as silent partners until they returned in 1976.[14]

When the Bullards returned from Nigeria, the Tafoyas created their own cross-country supply business called All Family Sports. Jan Tafoya and Mary Ellen Magnus created the Bill Koch Ski School, which later became the Magnus Cross-Country Ski School.[15] They named it after the 1983 Cross-Country World Cup champion, Bill Koch.[16]

The early trails on the mountain were pretty informal. Most often, skiers plotted them through the woods and then skied down to an existing path, which they then followed. One popular trail went out to the K2 tower and then back west from there on trails that had been in use for years. As Bob Matson described, "Slowly but surely, they came up with some trails. The first ski trails weren't ski trails. They skied them in. He got them army wooden skis, and that's how they started."[17]

For many years, the Casper Nordic Ski Club had an agreement with Camp Sacajawea, the Girl Scouts camp on the western end of the mountain. In exchange for being allowed to train and race the high school team on camp property, the club maintained trails that the Girl Scouts could use in their summer camp. They also cut firewood for the campers to use during the summer. The club ran and skied the trails to pack them, and then raced on the narrow trails through the camp. This was quite inflexible, because the trails were narrow. This limited the training they could provide because the camp managers would not let them cut trees at Sacajawea.

Harry Brubaker remembers those early days.

When I first started skiing, which was '78, we were skiing at Sacajawea. And the high school program had an agreement with Sacajawea to— it was all classic skiing, so the trees were three feet apart and you had a trail that meandered through the trees, through the forest, and god forbid if we cut down any trees, the Girl Scouts would go bananas. So, we didn't cut down anything.

So, that kind of limited us in the development of trails in the Sacajawea area because the Girl Scouts wanted to preserve it for their nature walks that they did in the summer with their girls, which was reasonable on their part. Our ski races were there too.[18]

According to Bob Matson, much of the grooming in the early 1980s was done by Elmer Kandt. He would go up once a week and pack down the trails. After a snow, he did what was called "skiing a track in," which meant defining and packing it by skiing over it. The coaches worked on the trails in the same way. Later, they also began to groom the trails using snowmobiles.[19]

Creating the Modern Nordic Trails

With interest increasing in the 1970s, the Casper Nordic Ski Club began to rework the trails that were once central to Bumps-a-Daisy. They planned that the trail would curve to the east of the parks road and then head through the woods toward the Nursery slope. This interest in cross-country skiing was part of a growing movement to have a different kind of skiing experience that would appeal to both families and local ski teams, as well as to more hardcore skiers. It also came out of skiers' desire to do more ski skating. Classic style could use a three-foot-wide trail, but skating required a wider trail. When Bob Matson was describing cross-country competitive skiing, he got into talking about technique, which led to a discussion of why they moved the trails from Camp Sacajawea.

A lot of races, they'd start in classic style. A lot of them started with an uphill; that's how they used to sort out the field in those World Cup cross-country ski races. So, their first 2Ks were basically uphill. They had tape on the bottom of their skis with the wax in

it. They'd get up to the top of the hill, they'd pull the wax off and away they'd skate.

But there weren't any skating skis. They were just classic skis at that time. Then what we did was cut the tips off; so, the javelin tips, everybody cut them so they were rounded. Then they didn't get hung up. But being a double camber ski, it was still really awkward. The tips got caught all the time. And that's how we got started over at the county trail system. We'd got to the point where we were going to have to skate, and everybody really did want to skate. The Girl Scouts weren't going to have it, and that's not really great terrain anyway over there for skating.[20]

They groomed the snow on the trails in the winter, and during the summer, the trails doubled as hiking paths. Over time, users included fat-tire bikers and snowmobilers in the winter and mountain bikers and hikers in the summer.

Matson explained how they decided to go back over to Bumps-a-Daisy. "When we started skiing over there, I can remember him [Dave Martin]— he and old Bob Adams, I got a call at school that said, 'C'mon up.' And they had that bug tree study on the mountain at that time. That's how the Maze got cut like that. I showed up and Dave said, 'What's this look like?' I said it looks like ski trails to me. He said, 'Well, I started this. It's going to be a battle to start with.' And Bob Adams knew. So, we didn't have much."[21]

For many years, the Natrona County Parks Department had been unwilling to get involved in improving the 1930s vintage Nordic trails. In addition to the work that the ski club had taken on, Dave Martin, a worker with the parks, decided to begin reworking existing trails that ran through parks land. Martin and his team made some of the biggest improvements in the trails.

David (Dave) Martin is the son of Mary and Bud Martin. Mary was the oldest daughter of Neal Forsling and Don Ogilbee. Dave grew up in Rapid City, South Dakota. He married Jan in 1980. In the late 1970s, he built and lived in a cabin on Casper

Mountain that was on land that he got from his grandmother Neal. Dave's cabin burned in 2012 in the Sheepherder Hill fire. He later sold the land.

In the winter of 1975–76, he moved to Casper Mountain and began to cut the logs for his cabin. He had two guys from Minnesota with him, helping him with the cabin. They skied at Crimson Dawn. As they cut the logs, they skidded them out while on their skis. In the fall of 1977, he worked in Bruce Lamberson's Hogadon ski shop. To get to work or go to town, he skied out from his cabin, down the old Crimson Dawn road, and then to the Circle Drive, where his truck was parked. Then, he would go to work at Hogadon. He generally got in three miles of cross-country a day.[22]

These modern signs replaced Dave Martin's old, yellow directional markers. *(Casper Nordic Ski Club collection)*

Beginning in 1977, he worked for the Natrona County Parks Department, with parks director Bob Adams. When Dave approached Bob about improving trails, Bob told them they already had trails but that nobody used them. So, Dave checked out the trails and figured out how to improve them. Dave took it upon himself to work with another employee, in the winter, to work on the existing trails and to add others. They skied around on the overgrown trails and started cutting with a chain saw. First, they dug down into the snow; then, they cut down trees, set them aside, and then marked the newly widened trails with small, yellow blocks of wood, nailed to the trees. They created the markers by taking yellow road paint and painting it on wood chunks created as they cut down the trees. These were not regulation markings but were cheap to make and eventually evolved into a better system. And when people started using the new and improved trails, he got permission to continue to thin existing trails and to cut new ones. Their first projects were what are now called the Skunk Hollow and Strube Loop trails.[23]

They also connected to Beartrap Park. The next year, they extended the trail to what they called the North Forty, which was up on Tower Hill. There were also a number of unofficial, improvised trails, where people just started using a route and then others followed. Initially, Dave Martin did most of this under the radar, without formal parks department approval. When the trails became popular, the parks administration was able to take the credit.[24]

Building the Maze

Bob Matson mentioned that the section of trail called the Maze was part of Sam Weaver's pine beetle study area. Sam had gotten a grant to study the effect of mitigation on the rising level of pine beetle damage in western US forests. To gather data, they initially sectioned off the area of the county parks that was in the old Bumps-a-Daisy ski area. They marked off sections and thinned timber in some, leaving others pristine. That created a winding set of narrow pathways through the woods. Some of them intersected the trails Dave Martin had been working on.[25]

At times, Martin had to be creative to get the work done. Years before, when he was living in Minnesota, he had gotten started with skiing in the mid-1970s, taking Minnesota Department of Corrections juvenile offenders out on winter cross-country ski camping trips. Matson provided insight into how that experience gave Dave an idea for getting workers to help him. Cutting the trees produced a lot of slash. To get it cleared, Dave worked out a deal with the sheriff's department to have prisoners do the work.

There was a whole lot of slash, so the first people that hauled that slash out, they were the high school kids. They earned their keep to ski up there. But they had some guys from the jail up there. And he [Martin] had them up there for about a month. They'd bring these guys up and they would pull slash and stack logs and do all that kind of stuff too.

I can remember he called me up: "Matson, you gotta get up here for this. This is going to be— you're going to see people really happy to stay up here and work their butts off." So, I buzzed up there after school. And they had the guys out there, the old deputies were there. And Dave had them lined up. He said, "Okay, you have two choices. One, go back downtown or, two, keep coming up here for about two or three weeks, and we'll build a real nice warming hut right here. How many are for it?" And those guys [laughs] were all excited. And that's why it's called Martin's Hut. It was built right there. I think the ski kids put linseed oil on that for years.[26]

Dave Martin also donated an exterior door and a wood heating stove for the hut. So, naming the hut after him must have seemed logical.

The North Forty

Another section of the trails began to take form at about the same time. Again, Matson provides insight.

But the other part is up in what they call the North Forty. That was cut kind of the same way. There were trails and cross trails. They were connected by one trail, and that's the old Bumps-a-Daisy trail that goes up. You get up there on top and there's a road that goes around the ridge trail. That's kinda how that got started.

So, there was only one way up and one way down. So, the early skiing there was pretty dangerous because you only had one way to come down. Some people weren't real good skiers and it's really easy to lose control in a hurry. So, we had several accidents there, as well as accidents from tubing on the ski jump hill there.

But the county really worked with us and the public to get things safe. We started marking and developing other trails. Trails that go up and down. So that whole trail system has been marked out over time.

Dave Martin was a big part of that. He actually marked a lot of the back country trails, which are now the bike trails, mountain bike trails up there. He was a big proponent of that. And Doyle [Mangus] and I.

There were some real characters. People just kinda did it. And the county was really good about helping us out. We did a lot of the work, but they did a lot of the cleanup for us, like taking out the stumps and doing that sort of thing. But it was a real community project.[27]

A final piece of the trails system came from an agreement between the Bishop family and the Casper Nordic Ski Club. The Bishops owned property east of and adjacent to the main road, ending near Wa-Wa Lodge. They agreed to allow skiers to come onto their land for skiing. Their only condition was that people not come on the property during the summer because the family was up there in the warm months and liked their seclusion.[28]

A major problem faced by the Nordic club was that trail planning and construction cost money, as did seasonal maintenance. The county commissioners and the parks board had to be convinced that this was work worth paying for. And there were, frankly, many competing recreational programs on the mountain and at Alcova Lake, which all needed their share from the county coffers.

Bob Adams was the political brains of the county parks system. As the director, he had to convince tight-fisted commissioners that each program warranted an investment of county funds. Dave Martin and his colleagues would not have been able to do the work they did without Bob at the helm. Early on in his career, Adams had moved a small A-frame from Alcova Lake. The building became a storage site and a 1950s warming hut at Skunk Hollow. It later ended up as the first ski patrol building at Hogadon.

Bob was a year-around resident of Casper Mountain. He and his first wife, Carol, lived in one of the cabins at the bottom of Nursery, one that had been built by Ole Fougstedt. After Bob and Carol divorced, he built a geodesic dome below Wa-Wa Lodge, overlooking Elkhorn Canyon. It was on land purchased from the Cummings and Street families. Bob, his new wife, Ann, and their children lived in the dome.

Initially, Bob was a high school teacher, but he wanted to do more to improve the mountain. He quit teaching, went to work as the county parks director, and was in charge of the mountain and the lake parks. One of Bob's signature projects was the archery range on the western end of the mountain, near Camp Sacajawea. He also worked to get approval for the East End Road that became a new access point for landowners around Crimson Dawn; it also became an important conduit for the Nordic trails and, later, for the Casper Mountain Biathlon Center.

Again, Bob Matson provided insight regarding Bob's role.

> Then Bob Adams, he was really good. I think Bob did more, for my mind, did more for Casper Mountain recreation, with the archery range— he really

thought ahead. And he looked at me, said, [laughs] "We'll kind of get this started, and nobody's going to like it. But once the commissioners start getting phone calls about how great the county is for providing that up there, you're in." The development of this whole thing will be kids on skis. And that's been the story. If it wasn't for kids on skis, there wouldn't be, it wouldn't be. That's what got things going.[29]

As more and more people saw the mountain as a desirable place for outdoor recreation, competing interests sometimes placed different demands on the same land. Grooming for a ski trail was different for casual skiers than for racers. Snowmobilers would also use the trails, which ruined the surface for skiing. In the summer, hikers, bicyclers, people on four-wheelers, and casual walkers all had a different view of trail use. The problem became one of creating multiuse trails and then educating users so that they collaborated—rather than competed—on the tracks.

Dorothy Bullard described the tensions that arose between snowmobile enthusiasts and the cross-country skiers.

> There began to be conflicts on Casper Mountain between snow mobile enthusiasts and the X-C skiers. During the late '70s and '80s, we were on the verge of all-out war with snow machiners threatening skiers who were in their way. They did not like to slow down or be startled by skiers who obviously could not travel as fast. The county parks folks became concerned about possible confrontations so they divided the area around Bear Trap to keep the two groups separated. This separation eventually brought about the formation of the X-C trails system in and around the Strube Loop area. The Maze was a network of trails on the hill in the middle of Strube Loop where there was a warming hut. Skiers could start a fire, have a picnic or just get warm.[30]

Bob Matson also had some insight on how this was resolved.

Of course, at that time, it was a battle because the snow machines thought, "Oh, great, now we have some trails." Big Trail started at— it's the bottom, we call it the Beartrap Trail that goes up towards the meadow. And there weren't any trails up above. That was the snow machine trail along the road, if you ski up there. Ski down through there, and then you'd go up and then down Miller's Hill. The old trail went across the road, so it came down from Beartrap, down along there, and along the road, and then down Miller's Hill, and then up behind the county building. And then it went down to the old Wa-Wa Lodge. Then Strube Loop was the snow machine trail.

We had a meeting, negotiated a pact with the snow machine guys. And they were really good about it. Basically, it was that the ski trails would be on the east side of the road there, and then the snow machine trails would basically be on the other side. And that worked out really well.

To start with, on that Strube Road, we had the snow machines on one side and the skiers on the other. But slowly but surely, it got to where we had a ski trail system and a snow machine trail system.[31]

The Casper Nordic Ski Club also needed to acquire better grooming equipment. Bob Matson recalled how Dave Martin, who was now in charge of grooming trails and keeping parks roads open, managed to create the first packer. "He got a surplus tractor, and I believe he got that from the forest service. And Dave was really handy. So, we welded the iron thing that we hooked on with a chain in the back. That was the groomer. So, you can imagine what that was like [chuckles]. That was the first kind of packed trail set we had."[32]

Packing the trails in 2017 *(Casper Mountain Parks collection)*

Left: **Better packers make it possible to create wider trails, useable by casual skiers, racers, and others.** *(Photograph by Cathy Holman)* Right: **Packing with the Casper Nordic Ski Club's Arctic Cat. This is also used to pack at the Biathlon Center.** *(Casper Nordic Ski Club collection)*

Harry Brubaker, another member of the Casper Nordic Ski Club, recalled when they got their first new trail packer.

> Then Lee Burgess came in. He filled the hole for about eighteen months. Then I think he retired. Then Joe [Gillingham] came in. The Casper Nordic Club, we convinced the county that we had enough people skiing on the mountain and selling ski passes—that's about when that came in—that we could defray the cost of a $40,000 PistonBully to have a professional grooming machine up there. And that thing lasted— we still have it and they've rebuilt it. But they don't use it all that much because it's a small machine. We had to widen the trails from the ten or twelve feet wide to about fifteen feet to accommodate the PistonBully.[33]

Bob Matson ended his interview with a comment on how the development of the cross-country trails had been a community effort:

I just think that anything that's happened up there is the result of a lot of people jumping in. Way back when, people just took jobs that appealed to them. Don Jacobson was the champion of the lights. Jimmy [Miller] and I became the champion of race trails and the racing part of it, obviously, the coaching. And Harry, with his construction background, took on the facility with the energy he had. Everybody just jumped in. Nobody walked on each other's feet. Everybody just pitched in.[34]

Nordic Ski Patrol

MaryAnn Hoff began our discussion of the Nordic Ski Patrol.

> Then the other part of it was the Nordic patrol. So, you trained, you could be on both patrols. You could be on the Nordic and the Alpine. So, we'd train over there too. Rescue. Figuring out how to rescue somebody, how to handle a toboggan that could be taken to the scene of an accident over in the Nordic area.
>
> They had a storage place over there where you could keep your supplies. So, that was a big part

of the patrol too. And then during the day, there wasn't anybody patrolling over there. So, if they had an accident, they'd call the patrol and we'd take a toboggan or something over to help them out at the Nordic. But people don't get injured as bad at the Nordic as they do, it seems like, the Alpine.[35]

When Sandy Leotta and MaryAnn Hoff interviewed Bill and Jan Chambers in 2019, they discussed building a patrol for Nordic skiing on the mountain. Bill remembered that Everett Akam, Stan Lowe, and Craig Carlson had been some of the people getting a cross-country patroller system going. Bill noted that there still was not a regular Nordic patrol but that a few of the Hogadon patrollers were cross listed for Nordic. They included Sean Ellis, Sam Weaver, and Kent Doing, who would do a circuit to make sure that there were no injuries.[36]

Bob Matson laid some of the credit on Sam Weaver, who he said worked to bring both trained patrollers and their training to the Nordic trails. He noted that Sam was a regular patroller on the cross-country trails in the early years and was a serious champion for general public access to the trails.[37]

The rest of the conversation centered around how complicated the trail system had gotten to be. They noted that if someone got lost, they could call in and give a marker number, then someone would come in on a snow machine to guide them out. Sandy mentioned that no one had gotten lost for a few years. But MaryAnn reminded her that Craig Kittleson had just gotten lost a few weeks earlier. This was in 2019.[38]

Club and School Racing Programs

While there was continued interest in cross-country after World War II, the main emphasis was on expanding downhill slopes, culminating in 1959 in Hogadon Ski Area. The one exception was in high school sports. Natrona County High School (NCHS) initially had only a downhill club but, eventually, added cross-country. Anker Larson, who was coaching Alpine with Bill Haines at NCHS, was not keen on also having a cross-country team. When Kelly Walsh High School (KWHS) opened in 1964,

Don Jacobson (*Jacobson family collection*)

they wanted ski teams as well. That would come later in the decade with the arrival of Don Jacobson.

Don Jacobson, an electrical engineer, moved to Casper from Sheridan in the mid-1960s. He had learned to cross-country ski in the Big Horn Mountains and was delighted to continue that sport on Casper Mountain. During the 1969–70 school year, he helped start the cross-country ski team at NCHS. Like the downhill ski teams at NCHS, Nordic was a club team, not a formal school program. Don Walcott, who coached downhill at KWHS, worked with Jerry Overton who, in turn, recruited Don Jacobson to coach cross-country at Kelly Walsh. Over the years, the Alpine and Nordic teams trained and traveled to meets together. Don Jacobson's arrival helped raise Nordic skiing to an actual team sport at KWHS in 1970.[39] Jacobson coached at KWHS until 1974, though his contributions to cross-country continued until his death in 2014.[40] Each year, the student athletes now compete, in his honor, in the Don Jacobson Memorial High School Nordic Ski Meet.

After retiring, Jacobson spent time improving the cross-country trails. He used his electrical engineering skills to design a lighting system that would open up one kilometer of the trails to night skiers. He then found the money—including from an optional 1 percent tax fund—to get it built. And, of course, he oversaw the team that installed the lights.[41] Later, he and his wife, Susan, paid for a new and improved Jacobson's Hut in the North Forty area of the Nordic runs on Tower Hill.[42]

Bob Matson became the KWHS coach in 1981. Matson learned to ski during college in Minnesota, but he really became a ski enthusiast while living in the Black Hills of

Jim Miller and Bob Matson getting ready for a day on the trails. *(Jim Miller collection)*

South Dakota. His wife, Barb Marcom, came from a family that had developed the Bald Mountain Ski Club near Lead. After he arrived in Casper, he learned cross-country from Keith Tyler and Doyle and Mary Ellen Magnus.[43]

Bob shared a list of who had coached the Nordic teams between the 1970s and his start in 1981. He said that in 1974, Carol Spickard followed Don Jacobson at KWHS. She had gotten her start working with the Nordic team at NCHS. She was then in charge of the program at both schools. She moved to coaching only at NCHS and Morgan Smith took over at KWHS. After Smith was Joe Filer, then Scott Weber, and then Matson. When he took over, there were nine students on the team. After the district agreed to support the program for a few more years, they managed to turn it around.[44] During that same time, Jerry Hand, who was a science teacher, took on the NCHS Nordic program. According to Jim Miller, Bob Matson was the NCHS coach when Jim began to coach the KWHS team in 1991.[45]

The best description of Jim Miller comes from Bob Matson.

Then Jimmy [laughs] Miller came along and that was the real crank-up time. Jim had been an international-class skier, qualified for three Olympics, skied in two.

I'll tell you a story about Jim. He and his brother Pat, who was a heck of a skier, came from the Chisholm Ski Club back in Maine, a premier Nordic ski training facility and program. Anyway, he and his brother Pat had that Olympic background, so when they had the Olympics in Salt Lake, they asked me to come along with him. And we went to the reunion dinner for the Nordic combined guys from

Top: Larissa Gray, a junior at Natrona County High School, warms up with the Casper Nordic Ski Team in 2013. *(Casper Star-Tribune; photograph by Ryan Gorgan)* Bottom: The Casper High School Nordic Ski Team poses for a picture on the way to a meet in Jackson, Wyoming. *(Casper Nordic Ski Club collection)*

Jim and brother Pat Miller wax their Nordic skis. (*Jim Miller collection*)

classic skiing, he made Casper skiers and later Wyoming skiers and later Intermountain skiers, outside of probably New England, probably the best classic skiers in the country. Jim was a big part of that. Just his energy and willingness to just jump in there. That made the difference. That brought the energy that really propelled the program on.[46]

There have been other coaching changes in the twenty-first century. In 2014, Cassidy Jerding took over the Nordic program at Kelly Walsh High School. That same year, Justin Kinner came on as the coach for Natrona County High School. They took up the helm from Jim Miller and Bob Matson, who both moved down to be assistant coaches. Both Kinner

Jim Miller collected examples of all of the skis he ever used. (*Jim Miller collection*)

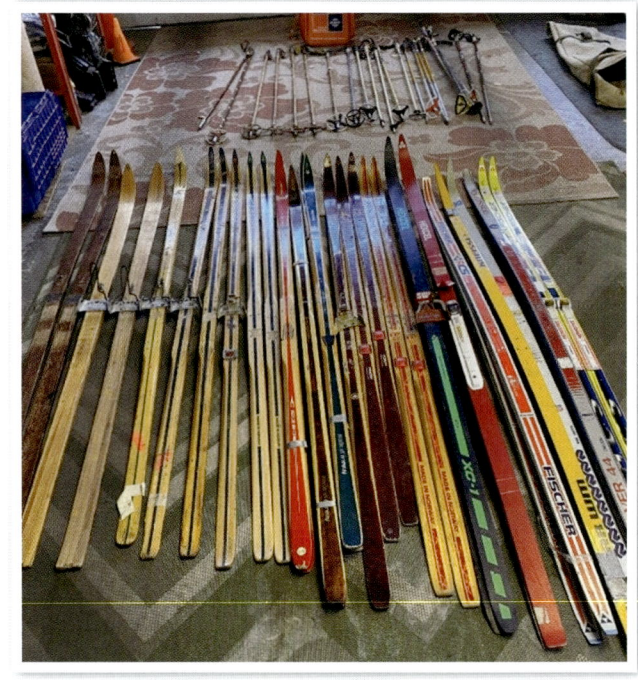

all those years. I'll tell you what, you talk about a stable full of crazy people. But it was really fun.

I got to get around and talk to some of these guys. I knew the coach from Norway from when Barbara and I went to school over there. We were talking about skiers and who they thought was best in their era. And there were several of those guys. It was Gunderson from Norway and the Swedish guy and a Russian guy and a Czech guy, that said—they were the old-timers still coaching and hanging on—they said that in his day, Jim Miller was the best skier in the world. He won't tell you this, but I know because I wrote up his deal to get him in the national hall of fame.

He qualified for every ski event except biathlon. He could have been on the national Olympic team for all those ski events. That's all the Alpine events and flat-track cross-country skiing events. Plus, ski jumping. But he was in Nordic combined that combined the best of both. He'll never say anything about it and he's real low profile. But having him come on. He really provided, particularly with

and Jerding had been college champion skiers and had spent the previous five years as parent volunteers and coaches. They felt they had learned most of what they knew by working with the older coaches.[47]

One challenge of coaching Nordic has been building a program. The newest coaches have benefitted from planning by Don Jacobson, Bob Matson, and Jim Miller. In response to an interview question, Miller described how they finally got middle and high school students to join the Nordic teams.

Jim: I think we just had fun at it. We loved to do it. I love kids. And I felt like with my experience in the past being on the Olympic team for two different years, that I needed to give back to the community. I couldn't be back in Rumford, Maine, but I thought if I could take it and bring it to Casper, then I thought I just had to do that. It was something that was a passion of mine, and I loved it.

Sandy: How many kids were on the team when you started?

Jim: Oh, golly. A handful, maybe ten kids. Didn't matter. If it was one kid, it was fine.

Sandy: Then how did more kids come on? Was it word of mouth? Did you do something?

Jim: It was word of mouth, and I think kids heard that it was a lot of fun. I've coached many sports. And anything that I've coached, I made it fun. If I don't make fun, then it's not fun for the kids. So, I think word of mouth spread that way. I coached soccer and I coached cross-country running. And recruited heavily from them. Bob recruited football players from NC. Wrestlers. It was amazing how many different sports kids were coming out and saying, "We want to ski."

Knowing that they didn't have any skis, but we told them, don't worry, we'll find them. We begged, borrowed and wrote grants on getting enough equipment so everyone could ski.

These Casper High School Nordic Ski Team racers are competing during the 2021 season. *(Photograph by Tory Radosevich)*

MaryAnn: Who wrote the grants and who were some of the players that got those skis?

Jim: Bob wrote a grant for the Natrona County rec board. He wrote the first grant—and it might have been the only way—that we received X amount of pairs of skis. Basically, it was for elementary kids. We thought that's the way to build the program, is to have younger kids get involved. Then, the parents would get involved, therefore on up the line.

So, on that grant, we got a bunch of fish scales that elementary kids could ski on. We opened it up to any of the elementary schools. If their PE program or a class wanted to come to ski, we'd teach them how to ski.[48]

For the uninitiated, fish scales go under the center of the bottom of a ski. They provide traction to help get up hills and to not slide down backwards.[49]

Left: These students take Nordic ski lessons through the Magnus Ski School. *(Photograph by Tori Radosevich)* Bottom: Della Works prepares to take a group of young cross-country skiers down the trail. *(Della Works collection)*

Another ongoing program is Special Olympics racing. The two photos below show racers getting ready to go and then the award ceremony afterwards. The race took place in 2021 as a prelude to going to the state competition.

Top: **Winners of the 2021 Special Olympics receive their trophies.** Bottom: **In 2021, Special Olympics held its annual cross-country race.**

These students are participating in an elementary school Nordic class. (*Casper Nordic Ski Club collection*)

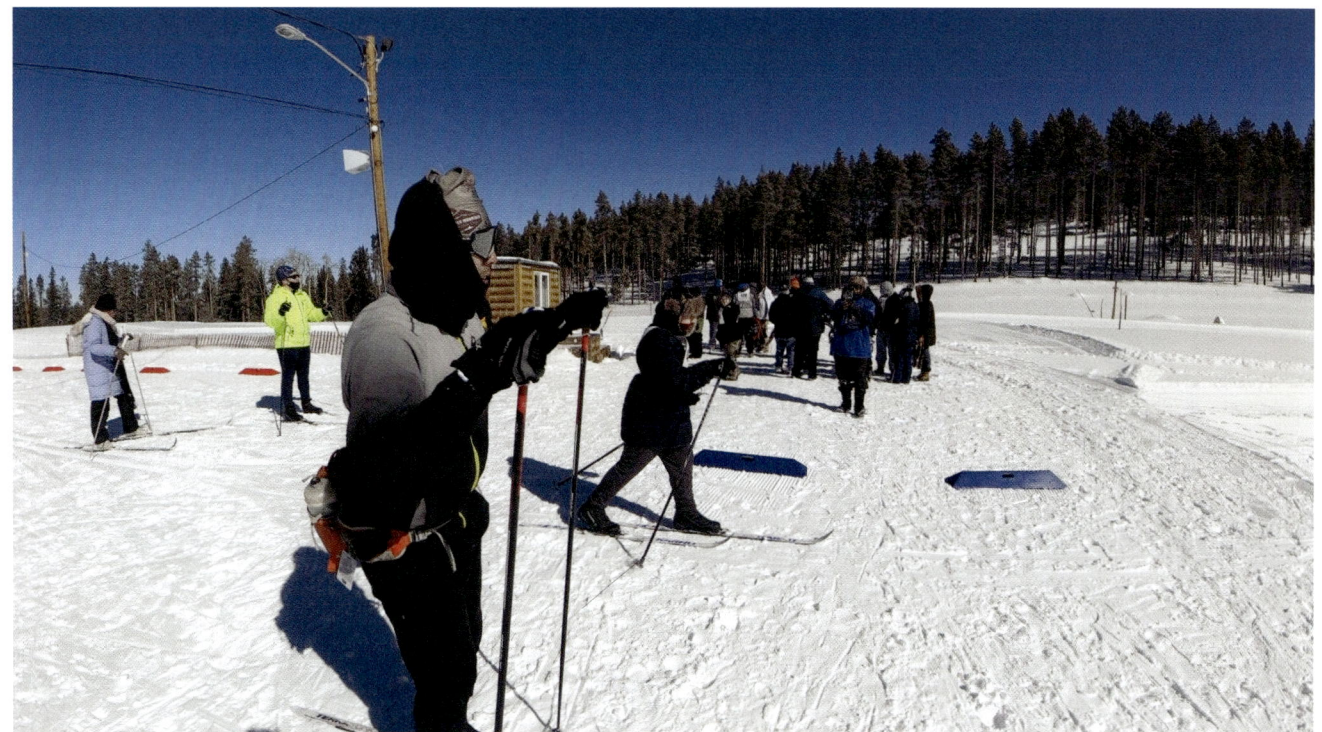

The Casper Mountain Trails Center

In the 1990s, Bob Matson invited Harry Brubaker to help coach the Casper Nordic Ski Team. Harry had grown up in Colorado and had been a runner and skier for decades. He had been working with youth cross-country racers on the mountain since 1974. And, he has been a continuing force in bringing more people to cross-country skiing.

He also participated in and then taught in the National Guard biathlon program. This required him to attend a number of National Guard training seminars, during which he learned a lot about the physiology of racing. He raised interest in and helped get the land to create the Casper Mountain Biathlon Center on the East End Road.

In addition to teaching, Harry made other important contributions to the growth of Nordic skiing. He designed and found funding for building the Cross-Country Lodge just uphill to the west of Skunk Hollow. Harry shared his story about the construction of the Casper Mountain Trails Center.

> So, my deal— well, I was a contractor all my life and I was also ski coach. I said, "Well, I'll just build us a lodge." So that's when I got ahold of Kelly Estes. He was the parks dude at the time. I said, "Kelly, we've been wanting a lodge now for the last fifteen years up here. County keeps saying yeah, yeah, yeah." No headway was done on it.
>
> So, Kelly and I, we went up and we identified six locations that we thought would be good for a lodge. And we got a backhoe. Ben Brown up there on the top of the mountain had a backhoe, and he supplied it to us free of charge. We dug a hole to see what the dirt was like underneath and how far it was down to the rock and sand and all that. Out of the six locations, we chose the one where the lodge is built right now.
>
> We dug the foundations down— you got about two feet of ten million years of pine needles making topsoil. You go through that two feet and then you hit this rocky, sandy stuff. I felt that was suitable for holding up a log cabin, the size of a log cabin.
>
> So, once we identified it and we hold the bulldozer standing by right there. We bulldozed out where we wanted the building. And the day that he said this is it, we bulldozed it and I poured concrete that day—so that nobody could change their mind. I didn't have a permit. I didn't have a plan. Didn't have anything. Well, I had a plan in my head, and we built that whole lodge out of my head. Didn't have a plan. It's twenty-eight feet wide and seventy-two feet long. I knew that the walls were going to be about ten feet high. And I knew that the trusses were going to be every nine feet. That's why it ended up being seventy-two foot because that's a multiple of nine. So that's how it was built.
>
> Four years later, after six thousand hours of volunteer labor from the Nordic Club, John Bailey, the plumber, he donated all the plumbing—his time was donated. Casper Electric donated their time. We got a deal on the logs; they were $40,000 for the log kit. We didn't have to cut one single log—that came in as a kit from Missoula, Montana. Real Log Homes supplied that. And they gave us a break on price on that because it was for us, a 501(c)(4). We didn't have to pay tax on it because the Nordic club bought it.
>
> But we built that. We broke ground in 2000, and by 2004, we dedicated it. One of the commissioners came up and said, "I didn't even know you were building this damn thing. Did you ever take out a permit on this?" "No." "Well, you shouldn't have done that!" But we got our lodge.[50]

Jim Miller noted how building the lodge was, once again, a community project. "So, we all had a hand in it. Building, hammer and nails, screws. The club— I can remember a lot of the ladies said, 'We'll get up on that scaffolding inside and do the tongue and groove, and we'll put everything together.' It just came together. I was like, 'How? How can that happen?' County got involved with electrician work. It was a huge community effort, which was basically orchestrated by the ski club." Sandy Leotta asked who some of the women were. Jim said, "The ski club, we have Tori Radosevich and Nina DeVore. My wife, Pam. If we need something, they just go do it."[51]

As part of the building process, the county made them alter the plans to include water, indoor toilets, and a kitchen. All of that, in the future, allowed the building to be a rental hall and even a small restaurant. The center became a community center for the mountain, as well as the starting point for racing and casual gatherings.

In 2010, it was also the site of a celebration of life for Buck Weaver, one of the old mountain skiing pioneers. Over 250 skiers, townies, and mountain residents crowded into the hall to say farewell. Buck had been one of the few old timers left who had helped build up skiing from a one-hill scene to what it was in the 2000s. It was the end of an era.

The Nordic lodge came to a sad end in 2020. Water damage from structural problems left it leaky and moldy, so the county decided it would be cheaper to tear it down and build a

Skiers gather outside of the Casper Mountain Trails Center. *(Casper Nordic Ski Club collection)*

new center. The building came down in the fall of 2020. A temporary building is serving skiers and others through 2021 and part of 2022. The new lodge, built on the same site, should be ready for use by the 2022 cross-country season.[52]

Another job that the Casper Nordic Ski Club took on was the construction of storage buildings, one for senior high teams and one for junior high. They also undertook building an electronic scoreboard that would allow for more use by racers, including the Special Olympics racing program. Again, Jim Miller credited the large number of volunteers who made such things possible. Some of the names he mentioned were Rita Nelson, Laura McClury, and Terri Weiner.[53]

The Casper Mountain Biathlon Center

Harry Brubaker began working to get a biathlon center on Casper Mountain after he attended a national meet. He realized that this sport, which combines cross-country skiing and shooting, could bring both opportunities and money to the Casper area. The Casper Mountain Biathlon Club (CMBC) was led by a board of trustees that included Kathy and Rob Rosser, as well as Harry Brubaker. Kathy Rosser was the head of the Hogadon ski school until she met Rob and shifted her focus to biathlon.

The CMBC started out to raise $7 million. They needed the first $5 million to buy forty acres of land along the East

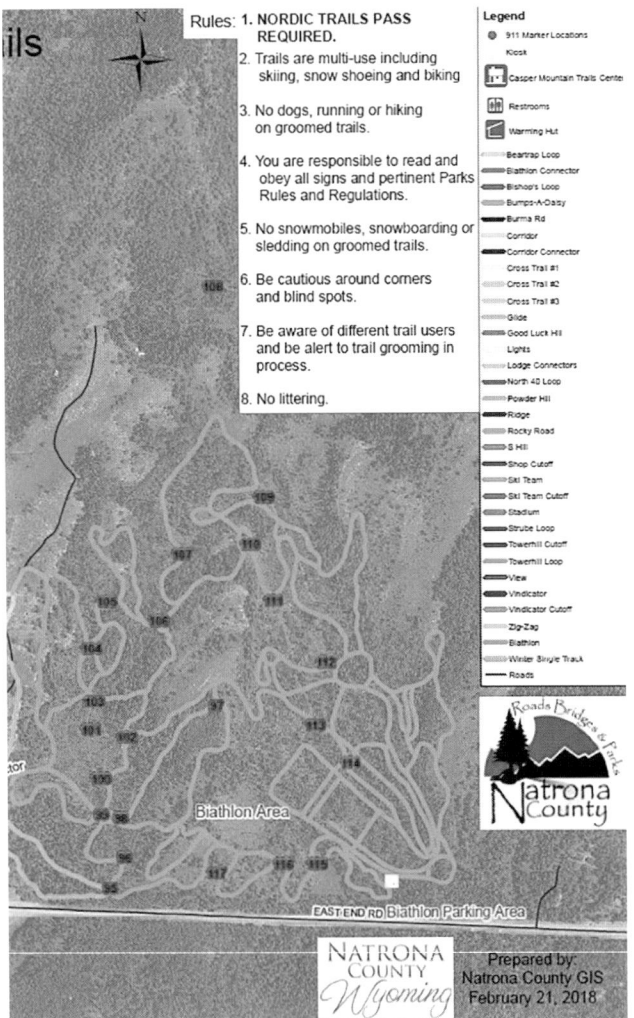

Left: This map lays out the trail system of the Casper Mountain Biathlon Center. *(Natrona County collection)* Right: This is the Casper Mountain Biathlon Center. *(CMBC collection)*

Left: Casper Mountain pioneer skiers Lucy Rognstad, Bud Stratton, and Lou Demorest enjoy the peace of a winter day as they pause in their cross-country route. *(Photograph by Jan Demorest)* Right: Buck, Cara, Sam, and Chris Weaver get in a little Nordic skiing near Sam's front yard on Casper Mountain. *(Laurie Weaver collection)*

End Road on the mountain. The McMurry Foundation, a Wyoming philanthropy supporting outdoor and social programs, especially in Natrona County, agreed to purchase the land. The foundation worked out a memo of understanding, with the county giving CMBC use of the land through a fifty-year lease.[54] The lease is renewable for another period after the fifty years expire. If it ceases to be a biathlon center, that can void the lease. And if the lease goes out of force, the land belongs to the McMurry Foundation.[55]

The CMBC then spent another million dollars on preparing the site and an additional million for all of the equipment. Finally, by 2016, they were ready to open for events and to be a training facility. From Harry Brubaker, in 2019:

> Well, the first event was three years ago, and it was a local event. The following year, we had a regional where the National Guards from about eighteen different states came in here and had a regional meet. Then we had the Korean women's biathlon team came in here last fall or last winter. They were going to stay a week, just to kind of check out

things. They stayed a month until the snow melted. It finally melted and they couldn't stay any longer; they left! But they loved it here.

> Then the Romanian team has been here and visitors from the Russian team and the German team and Norwegian team, they sent representatives here to check things out. So, they know it's here.[56]

The Casper Mountain Biathlon Center hosts numerous events for National Guard, national biathlon, and Paralympics groups. It has become one of the most versatile centers in the United States.[57]

As with the other skiing communities, the Nordic and biathlon communities have built their centers through the work of like-minded individuals who give time, labor, and money to make the mountain an outdoors destination. Many people just love to get out into the crisp mountain air and glide along smooth mountain paths. They can come to the cross-country trails for an outing. It has indeed proved to be a sport for both old friends and families alike.

Bill DeVore, Nina DeVore, Christy Garner, Tori Radosevich, Bridget Veauthier, Pam Miller, and Jim Miller at the 2018 Taste of Trails progressive dinner. Their Norse outfits reflect the event's Swedish theme. *(Casper Nordic Ski Club collection)*

Postscript

Dos and Don'ts of Casper Mountain's Nordic Ski Trails

DO: Buy your Trail Pass. You can get a single pass or a family pass from pretty much any local sports store or from Natrona County Parks. The money goes towards maintaining the trails and keeping them safe for us to use.

DON'T: Be a freeloader. I don't think it's a problem to bring a guest with you occasionally or to wait until you've used the trails once before investing in a pass. But if you're a frequent trail user buy your Trail Pass.

DO: Feel free to snowshoe on the Nordic Ski Trails, not just the single track that's specifically designated for snowshoers.

DON'T: Walk in the middle of the Ski Trail, try and keep off to the sides. There are two reasons for this. First, the snowshoes can cause divots and cuts in the groomed ski trails that make it harder for skiers. Second, it's a safety thing! Skiers gather a lot of speed on those hills and less experienced ones may not be able to move to the side or navigate around a large group of people.

DO: Fat Bike on either the Ski Trail or the Single Track.

DON'T: Leave tracks in the snow on the Ski Trail. If you can see tracks being made by your bike, it's probably too powdery for you to be up Fat Biking. It turns out icy packed snow is the best snow for fat bikers!

DO: Pay attention to your surroundings and it's generally understood that the slower person should move out of the way for whoever is going faster. An example: A leisurely

These skiers enjoy Swedish-inspired food at Jacobson's Hut as part of the Taste of Trails progressive dinner. *(Photograph by Tori Radosevich)*

snowshoer should move to the side for someone running with snowshoes, or a snowshoer should move aside for a skier.

DON'T: Have your music up so loud that you can't hear what's going on around you. Often skiers and fat-tire bikers will let out a warning when they are passing, you may become irritated or even get hurt if you don't hear them over your tunes.

DON'T: Allow your dog on the groomed Nordic Ski Trails.

DO: Enjoy the mountain, find your zen while getting a good workout and when in doubt error on the side of being polite![58]

NOTES

1. Neal Forsling, memoirs, 1964, 2.

2. Forsling, memoirs, 2.

3. Forsling, memoirs, 2.

4. Forsling, memoirs, 2.

5. Julie York, reminiscences.

6. Angus Morrison, Casper Mountain Ski History Project, oral history interview by Sam Weaver, April 7, 2009, 2.

7. Morrison, interview, 2.

8. Bob Matson, Casper Mountain Ski History Project, oral history interview by MaryAnn Hoff and Sandy Leotta, 2020, 2–3.

9. Matson, interview, 3.

10. Miles Hecker, obituary, *Casper Star-Tribune*, October 15, 2013.

11. Dorothy Bullard, "Cross Country Skiing: A History," unpublished story, December 2013, 1.

12. Bullard, "Cross Country Skiing," 1.

13. Matson, interview, 3.

14. Bullard, "Cross Country Skiing," 1.

15. Bullard, "Cross Country Skiing," 1.

16. Matson, interview, 4.

17. Matson, interview, 2.

18. Harry Brubaker, Casper Mountain Ski History Project, oral history interview by MaryAnn Hoff and Sandy Leotta, October 21, 2019.

19. Matson, interview, 3–4.

20. Matson, interview, 4.

21. Matson, interview, 5.

22. Dave Martin, Casper Mountain Ski History Project, oral history interview by MaryAnn Hoff and Sandy Leotta, 2019, 4–5.

23. Martin, interview, 2–3.

24. Martin, interview, 3–4.

25. Matson, interview, 5.

26. Matson, interview, 6.

27. Matson, interview, 7.

28. Brubaker, interview, 7–8.

29. Matson, interview, 6.

30. Bullard, "Cross Country Skiing," 3.

31. Matson, interview, 6.

32. Matson, interview, 5.

33. Brubaker, interview, 9.

34. Matson, interview, 14.

35. MaryAnn Hoff, Casper Mountain Ski History Project, oral history interview by Sandy Leotta, September 22, 2020, 6.

36. Bill Chambers in Bill and Janet Chambers, Casper Mountain Ski History Project, oral history interview by MaryAnn Hoff and Sandy Leotta, January 31, 2019, 23.

37. Matson, interview, 7.

38. Bill and Janet Chambers, interview, 23–24.

39. Bob Matson, Casper Mountain Ski History Project, oral history interview by MaryAnn Hoff and Sandy Leotta, 2020, 2.

40. Matson, interview, 8.

41. Christine Peterson, "Peterson: Casper skier leaves lasting legacy," *Casper Star-Tribune*, July 10, 2014, 1.

42. Peterson, "Peterson: Casper skier leaves lasting legacy," 2.

43. Matson, interview, 1–2.

44. Matson, interview, 8–9.

45. Jim Miller, Casper Mountain Ski History Project, oral history interview by Sandy Leotta and MaryAnn Hoff, 2020, 1.

46. Matson, interview, 11–12.

47. Ryan Dorgan, "Kelly Walsh, Natrona County welcome new Nordic ski coaches," *Casper Star-Tribune*, December 16, 2014, 1–2.

48. Miller, interview, 3.

49. Author's explanatory note.

50. Brubaker, interview, 10–11.

51. Miller, interview, 8.

52. Brendan LaChance, "Casper Mountain Trails Center demolition underway; new lodge being designed," *Oil City News*, November 9, 2020, 1.

53. Miller, interview, 8–9.

54. Brubaker, interview, 19.

55. Keith Tyler via Harry Brubaker.

56. Brubaker, interview, 16.

57. Miller, interview, 10.

58. Cathy Holman, "Dos and Don'ts of Casper Mountain's Nordic Ski Trails," Townsquare Media, February 5, 2019.

Bibliography

ORAL HISTORIES

Barton, Ralph. Casper Mountain Ski History Project. Oral history interview by Sam Weaver. March 31, 2012.

Bochmann, Glenn. Casper Mountain Ski History Project. Oral history interview by Sam Weaver. April 25, 2011.

Bochmann, Pat. Casper Mountain Ski History Project. Oral history interview by Sam Weaver. April 25, 2011.

Bon, Bill. Casper Mountain Ski History Project. Oral history interview by Sam Weaver. November 10, 2013.

Brubaker, Harry. Casper Mountain Ski History Project. Oral history interview by MaryAnn Hoff and Sandy Leotta. October 21, 2019.

Bundy, Wayne. Casper Mountain Ski History Project. Oral history interview by Sam Weaver. March 13, 2011.

Chambers, Bill and Janet. Casper Mountain Ski History Project. Oral history interview by MaryAnn Hoff and Sandy Leotta. January 31, 2019.

Demorest, Janet. Casper Mountain Ski History Project. Oral history interview by Sam Weaver. August 11, 2011.

DeVore, Stan. Casper Mountain Ski History Project. Oral history interview by MaryAnn Hoff and Sandy Leotta. April 3, 2019.

Ellis, Frank (Pinky). Casper Mountain Ski History Project. Oral history interview by Sam Weaver. January 3, 2014.

Ellis, Jackie. Casper Mountain Ski History Project. Oral history interview by MaryAnn Hoff and Sandy Leotta. 2020.

French, Doug. Casper Mountain Ski History Project. Oral history interview by Sam Weaver and Sean Ellis. August 8, 2009.

Garberg, Bill. Casper Mountain Ski History Project. Oral history interview by Sam Weaver. August 22, 2016.

Grace, Lee, and Kathy Morton. Casper Mountain Ski History Project. Oral history interview by Sam Weaver. 2014.

Hardesty, Bob. Casper Mountain Ski History Project. Oral history interview by Sam Weaver and Sean Ellis. January 3, 2011.

Harshman, Pat. Casper Mountain Ski History Project. Oral history interview by MaryAnn Hoff and Sandy Leotta. February 5, 2019.

Hoff, Ken. Casper Mountain Ski History Project. Oral history interview by MaryAnn Hoff and Sandy Leotta. March 26, 2019.

Hoff, MaryAnn. Casper Mountain Ski History Project. Oral history interview by Sandy Leotta. September 22, 2020.

Horn, Barry. Casper Mountain Ski History Project. Oral history interview by Sam Weaver. April 27, 2013.

Huber, Mike. Casper Mountain Ski History Project. Oral history interview by MaryAnn Hoff and Sandy Leotta. March 26, 2019.

Kidd, Bob. Casper Mountain Ski History Project. Oral history interview by Sam Weaver. November 15, 2014.

Ladd, Bill. Casper Mountain Ski History Project. Oral history interview by Sam Weaver. November 22, 2014.

Ladd, Marilyn. Casper Mountain Ski History Project. Oral history interview by Sam Weaver. November 22, 2014.

Ladd, Bruce. Casper Mountain Ski History Project. Oral history interview by MaryAnn Hoff and Sandy Leotta. January 23, 2019.

Lamberson, Bruce. Casper Mountain Ski History Project. Oral history interview by MaryAnn Hoff and Sandy Leotta. n.d.

Leotta, Sandy. Casper Mountain Ski History Project. Oral history interview by MaryAnn Hoff. September 22, 2020.

Loghry, Donna. Casper Mountain Ski History Project. Oral history interview by Sam Weaver. October 24, 2019.

Martin, Dave. Casper Mountain Ski History Project. Oral history interview by MaryAnn Hoff and Sandy Leotta. 2019.

Matson, Bob. Casper Mountain Ski History Project. Oral history interview by MaryAnn Hoff and Sandy Leotta. 2020.

Miller, Jim. Casper Mountain Ski History Project. Oral history interview by MaryAnn Hoff and Sandy Leotta. 2020.

Morrison, Angus McCloud. Casper Mountain Ski History Project. Oral history interview by Sam Weaver. April 7, 2009.

Peak, Charlie. Casper Mountain Ski History Project. Oral history interview by Sam Weaver. October 30, 2016.

Schilling, Jerry. Casper Mountain Ski History Project. Oral history interview by Sandy Leotta and MaryAnn Hoff. January 2021.

Scifers, Barbara Raymond. Casper Mountain Ski History Project. Oral history interview by Sam Weaver. March 11, 2010.

Smith, Chris. Casper Mountain Ski History Project. Oral history interview by MaryAnn Hoff and Sandy Leotta. February 7, 2019.

Stroock, Tom. Casper Mountain Ski History Project. Oral history interview by Sam Weaver and Sean Ellis. n.d.

Stuckenhoff, Marge. Casper Mountain Ski History Project. Oral history interview by Sam Weaver. September 26, 2010.

Walker, Cam. Casper Mountain Ski History Project. Oral history interview by MaryAnn Hoff and Sandy Leotta. March 21, 2019.

Walters, Fred. Casper Mountain Ski History Project. Oral history interview by Sam Weaver. October 31, 2015.

Weaver, Laurie. Casper Mountain Ski History Project. Oral history interview by MaryAnn Hoff and Sandy Leotta. January 16, 2019.

Weaver, Warren (Buck). Interview by MaryAnn Hoff. n.d.

——. Casper Mountain Ski History Project. Oral history interview by Sam Weaver. November 15, 2009.

Wold, John. Casper Mountain Ski History Project. Oral history interview by Sam Weaver. July 23, 2010.

CORRESPONDENCE

Cowan, Jay. Multiple e-mails to Rebecca Hunt. December 2020 to April 2021.

Forsling Neal. Letter to Nellie Weir. Winter 1931.

French, Doug. E-mail to Jackie Ellis. August 11, 2009.

Kidd, Bob. E-mail communication with Rebecca Hunt.

York, Julie. E-mail to Rebecca Hunt. "Family reminiscences." February 27, 2019.

BOOKS AND NEWSPAPER/JOURNAL ARTICLES

Casper Tribune-Herald. December 1930.

Clark, Miles. "The Origins of Skiing? | 8,000 Years Ago." SnowBrains. Accessed March 19, 2018. www.snow-brains.com/the-origins-of-skiing-7000-years-ago/.

Colorado Ski and Snowboard Museum and Hall of Fame. "Father John Lewis Dyer – Inspiration – 1977." Accessed March 19, 2018. www.skimuseum.net/halloffame/hall_of_fame_details.php?HallOfFameID=4.

Dawson, Louis. "Mountaineering and Backcountry Skiing." The Backcountry Skiing Blog. Accessed February 25, 2018. https://www.wildsnow.com/backcountry-skiing-history/backcountry-skiing-ski-mountaineering-chronology/.

French, T. (Ted) R. Letter to the editor. *Casper Times*, 1939.

Hunt, Rebecca A. *Natrona County: People, Place, and Time*. Virginia Beach, VA: The Donning Company Publishers, 2011.

——. *Wyoming Medical Center: A Centennial History*. Virginia Beach, VA: The Donning Company Publishers, 2010.

Kirshman, Jeff. "Kelly Walsh, Natrona County welcome new Nordic ski coaches." *Casper Star-Tribune*, December 16, 2014.

Klimzcak, Natalia. "5,000-Year-Old Rock Carving Depicting Skier in Norway Destroyed by Youths." Ancient Origins. Accessed February 25, 2018. http://www.ancient-origins.net/news-history-archaeology/5000-year-old-rock-carving-depicting-skier-norway-destroyed-youths-006380.

Krichko, Kade. "China's Stone Age Skiers and History's Harsh Lessons." *The New York Times*, April 19, 2017.

Lund, Morten, Seth Masia, and Mike Brady. "A Short History of Skis." International Ski History Association. Accessed February 25, 2018. https://www.skiinghistory.org/history/short-history-skis-0.

"The Masked Cavaliers." *Casper Magazine* 3, no. 14 (February/March 1980).

"Memorial: Thaddeus Hovenden Walker '41." Princeton Alumni Weekly. June 11, 2008. Accessed November 9, 2020. https://paw.princeton.edu/memorial/thaddeus-hovenden-walker-%E2%80%9941.

Mokler, Alfred J. *A History of Natrona County, Wyoming: 1888–1922*. Chicago: The Lakeside Press, 1923. Reprinted as a Centennial Edition. Casper, WY: Mountain States Lithographing, 1989.

National Ski Patrol. Official website. Accessed August 27, 2020. https://nspserves.org/history/.

"New Slalom Course on Casper Mountain will relieve congestion." *Casper Tribune-Herald*, 1939.

"New Tow Placed on Mountain Run." *Casper Tribune-Herald*, 1948.

"Nils Fougstedt Taken by Death." *Casper Tribune-Herald*. December 1930.

Norman, Cathleen. *Loveland Ski Area: Colorado's Best-Known Secret*. Virginia Beach, VA: The Donning Company Publishers, 2014.

"Olaf Fougstedt is Dead at 82." *Casper Tribune-Herald*. April 4, 1960.

Pontti, John, and Kenneth Luostari. *Midwest Skiing: A Glance Back*. Chicago: Arcadia Press, 2000.

Saur, Lasse. *Norskeski – til glede of besvær*. Høgskolen i Finnmark, 1999.

Spring, Agnes Wright. "Winter Sports Opportunities For Wyomingites Abundant." *Wyoming Stockman-Farmer*, November 1939.

US National Ski and Snowboard Hall of Fame. "Roger Langley: Hall of Fame Class of 1958." Accessed August 27, 2020. https://skihall.com/hall-of-famers/roger-langley/.

Webb, Frances Seely. "Area on Casper Mountain offers relaxation from worldly cares." *Casper Star-Tribune*, n.d.

Index

About the Author

D**R. REBECCA A. HUNT IS A RECENTLY RETIRED** CU-Denver history professor, where she taught gender, immigration, and the history of the American West, as well as museum studies.

Rebecca wrote her doctoral thesis on the immigrant communities in northwestern Denver and Globeville. She has published two books on hospital history—one on Swedish Medical Center (2005) and one on Wyoming Medical Center (2011). *Natrona County: People, Place, and Time* also came out in late 2011.

Rebecca served as historian for *A Woman to Match a Mountain* (2008), a documentary on Neal Forsling, a Casper, Wyoming, homesteader, environmentalist, artist, and writer. Her current projects include *Urban Pioneers: Continuity and Change in Two Denver Immigrant Neighborhoods* and a biography of Neal Forsling.

This is Rebecca's fourth book published by The Donning Company Publishers.